LEADING WITH LIGHT

Leadership Best Practices for Clarity, Confidence, and Fulfillment in the Workplace

Randy Noe

LISA

Keep shining your light!

gratefully

Randy

Table of Contents

Leading With Light

A leader is one who knows the way,
goes the way, and shows the way.

John Maxwell

I've worked with thousands of leaders across all functional areas from a wide variety of industries, from global companies to small businesses. Having observed many examples, actions and behaviors of leadership excellence, I've seen what works in bringing out the best, and experienced many examples of leadership failures.

I've had the pleasure to serve leaders who have entrusted me as a sounding board and thinking partner, and invited me to come alongside supporting their professional growth and success. I've asked lots of curious questions, listened to their insights and lessons learned, as they opened their hearts and minds to share their leadership philosophy, styles, and approaches.

The following pages are best practices and simple tools, actions and behaviors observed from inspirational leaders that *will* enable *you* to grow as a leader. You will be more fully seen as your brightest and most authentic self, courageous in exploring new vistas, with tenacity pursuing goals and manifesting vision to reality.

1

You will build stronger relationships, grow in adaptability to navigate challenges and change, and build resilience learning and growing from setbacks and disappointments.

What does it mean to lead with light?

There is light in each of us. When leaders grow in their *self*-awareness, knowing *who* they are, what they want, and living their core values and strengths, light emerges from within and shines brightest.

Light itself also illumines the path for leaders to grow *situational* awareness of *where* they are in the moment, set goals and chart compass direction. Thereby opening up a channel of curiosity for learning, exploring, and discovery. Seeing light in others, leaders encourage and challenge others to shine their own lights to be their highest and best.

Archbishop Desmond Tutu once said, "Hope is being able to see that there is light despite all the darkness." Light and dark are always present. On the brightest sunny day there's a shadow, even the darkest nights have the moon and stars. When circumstances throw us off course, times are darkest or unclear, we can aim for light. Sometimes all we need to do to see light is lift our heads and hearts to look up.

YOU are a beacon of light.
Own it!

Light Provides Clarity

Clarity Breeds Confidence

Believe in yourself! Have faith in your abilities!
Without a humble but reasonable confidence in
your own powers you cannot be successful or happy.

Norman Vincent Peale

Light brings clarity that enables leaders to take positive action. When leaders know who they are (their individual identity), their core values and strengths, what they want and why, they can step with confidence and purpose. When leaders see where they are, what's around them, what they're doing, and the direction they're heading, they can make choices, set meaningful goals, and define boundaries.

With clarity of the organization's overarching mission, vision, values, and strategy, the leader's goals and intentions can be aligned. With clarity of organization and team goals, awareness of individual's strengths, hopes and dreams, leaders provide targeted guidance and direction. They can encourage, support, and challenge them.

Clarity breeds confidence.
Confidence infuses energy and enthusiasm to
act and communicate boldly for positive results.

The opposite of clarity is ambiguity. With less light there is less clarity, and more ambiguity. Ambiguity creates doubt, and doubt creates tension that tightens and shrinks, hinders progress and success.

Clarity accelerates a leader's growth, effectiveness, and fulfillment. Clarity enables leaders to stand and speak up with boldness for themselves and the team, and be the inspirational leaders they aspire to become.

Clarity Breeds Confidence
Reflection Questions

What are some statements that express who you are ("I am . . .", "I am not . . .")?

How do you describe yourself as a leader today?

What are your core values? What are your strengths?

What are your goals today? What do you want to achieve this year? What's on your longer term bucket list?

What are the goals of your team? What are the goals of each individual?

Who do you aspire to be as a leader?

Common Avoidable
Leadership Failures

*We see life through a filter that either blinds us
to all the beauty, wonder, and possibility
that surrounds us, or it brings them to light.*

Erwin Raphael McManus

What gets in the way from having a thriving, high performance culture? What hinders people from being fully engaged and contributing their highest and best? Often it results from all too common, and avoidable, actions and behaviors that result in derailing performance, lower engagement, and poor retention, including the following:

Over Alignment vs. Unleashing Talent

It is critical for all stakeholder participants to buy-in and align with a shared vision, mission, and core values. Like any strength, alignment can become a problem when overused. Beyond shared vision, mission, and values, alignment can become autocratic, command and control management that constrains creativity and innovation.

Leader unilateral declarations ("Either get on the bus, or get out!") and creeds ("It's my way or the highway!") stifle individual contribution. Do you want to encourage people to speak their minds and hearts, so they can develop and grow as leaders themselves? Are truth tellers with alternative points of view and different perspectives welcomed or discouraged?

Do you want a culture
of courage or compliance?
Do you want to unleash talent and empower,
or people to shut up and salute?

Unrealistic Expectations

Goal setting can become a problem when overused. Research shows there is a diminishing marginal return on trying to do too much, too fast, all at once. As the number of goals increases, people tend to accomplish less and less. One to three goals enables clarity of focus and likely to get them done. With four to ten goals, people are pulled in more directions and likely to accomplish only a few. When challenged with more than ten goals, concentration is fragmented, with so many competing and clashing priorities that little or nothing gets done.

When being over-stretched past a point of full capacity, people can feel like they are juggling balls and spinning plates all at the same time. How many goals or initiatives are you currently pursuing?

Developing Self-Narratives and Propaganda without Input and Ignoring Feedback

Developing strategy, managing a P&L, and making decisions from on high without regard for the potential impact on culture or customer is risky. Fixed, rigid thinking creates blind spots. A closed mind is not open to new learning. It can be unaware of key input and not receptive to feedback from stakeholders. Different perspectives and fresh ideas enable more fully informed thought and decision making. Additionally, successful team building is impacted when people are treated like they are disposable assets, or ignored, they either burn out or leave.

Is building rapport and strengthening relationships a priority? Are you more focused on driving an agenda, getting answers to questions, hearing what you want to hear, driving to a predetermined outcome and controlling the interview vs. building rapport and having a conversation?

Managing Tasks and Solving Problems (including People)

People spend years developing and honing technical subject matter expertise and excel at solving problems, often under intense time pressure with limited resource constraints. They become successful, but sometimes leave a trail of dead bodies in their wake with physically exhausted, mentally and emotionally drained team.

People are often treated like umpires in the workplace. They are easily identified and flagged when they make mistakes, and booed when they mess up, but otherwise are not noticed when performing their tasks with excellence throughout the game.

Subject matter experts are problem solvers. When it's what we know best, it's easy to look for and find problems in others, then dispense quick fix advice. Problems are the focus when reviewing work product, identifying areas where the team messed up and applying corrective measures for next time. If no problems are found, just close the file and move on to the next job. Opportunities are missed to build rapport by noticing excellence and acknowledging what worked well.

Growth and development are enhanced when a leader asks questions about next growth steps, provides constructive input to improve, and offers gratitude and praise for their contribution.

Public Criticism and Excoriations

Intense work pressures, aggressive forecasts, under performance, competing priorities and agendas, clashing leadership styles and personalities are among many factors that create and escalate tension in the workplace. Leaders can be tempted to defend themselves by lashing out in group settings where people are held to account in full view of their colleagues.

Using judgmental, blaming, shaming and accusatory language directed at a person's identity (who they are) can diminish the individual. More constructive feedback focusing on specific behaviors (what they did) shared in appropriate settings (in private) can lead to positive change. Trust builds over time, but breaks down in an instant and can be hard to repair when people launch personal attacks and openly criticize (or talk behind backs). When the "fight, flight, freeze" instinct gets triggered, individuals react by taking the bait and engaging (fight), withdrawing (flight), or hiding (freeze) by shutting down and being reluctant to risk sticking their necks out.

Is your feedback or criticism language focused on the individual's identity, or specific behaviors? Is your speech used to build up or tear down?

Bullying, Controlling, and Passive-Aggressive Behaviors

Bullying behavior shows up in many forms. There are explicit, confrontational, fist pounding displays of intimidation. Erratic, volatile behavior creates a climate of people walking on eggshells.

Controlling behavior, micromanagement, surfacing late negative surprises just before deadlines, scurrying and scrambling with substantial last minute changes, never arriving at "good enough" are several examples that exasperate, demoralize and deflate a team.

There are more subtle passive-aggressive forms. For example, when leaders demand action while providing ambiguous direction and little or no guidance, people are forced to "mind-read" and interpret both what is said and what is not said, take a best guess and respond, only to get rebuked over and over again. The default behavior becomes submissive, breeding a culture of order takers waiting to be told what to do. Are people clear about what is expected?

Like cattle branding or a tattoo, negative perceptions once formed are hard to remove and highly resistant to change. I know of a leader who raised a performance issue that occurred over six years prior as an example that a high potential leader was not ready for promotion. If the company culture and leadership has a long memory, past mistakes are not forgotten. People may see, and want, the benefits of a safer environment, but if they don't believe leopards can change their spots, they are skeptical and reluctant to open up and take risks. Are failures, mistakes, and disappointments tolerated? How long do you hold onto the past? How long is your memory?

Clearly there are some breaches of integrity, ethics, and trust that are lines in the sand, and not in synch with the values of the organization. Does the punishment fit the crime? How do you encourage healthy learning and growth? How are people acknowledged for responding to constructive feedback, working to address and change any derailing behaviors and development goals? What does it take to let people off the hook and wipe the slate clean? Is forgiveness a value for the organization?

Conflict-Avoidant Behavior

Using email for delivering negative feedback, performance reviews, and compensation adjustments under guise of being too busy or overcommitted is no excuse for blowing off difficult conversations. Absence is communication, a betrayal of leadership that marginalizes and dehumanizes the individual. It is exasperating when people are thirsting for information and kept in the dark. Silence is deafening.

Delivering information that significantly impacts the lives of people deserves the dignity of face to face, heart to heart, human interaction. Great leaders do not shrink from or avoid conflict when direct communication is required. Leadership often requires making tough business decisions that impact people's lives, sometimes even having to let people go.

Whenever leadership fails, the organizational culture is deemed unsafe, values are trampled upon, or a lack of trust occurs, individual and collective performance is diminished. Sustainable growth happens with heightened awareness of the current state, clarity of what's important, elimination of derailing behaviors, and intentional choice by individual leaders and teams to make positive changes going forward.

Common Avoidable Leadership Failures
Reflection Questions

How does the organization culture unleash talent, encourage and empower people to engage and grow? Is it a culture of courage, or a culture of compliance?

How many goals or initiatives is the organization, and are you, currently pursuing?

How does leadership prioritize building rapport and strengthening relationships?

How do leaders balance driving an agenda with having conversations?

How long is the organization's memory for failures, mistakes, and disappointments? Is forgiveness a value for the organization?

Being Curious and Less Certain

Never lose a holy curiosity.

Albert Einstein

Inspirational leaders lead with curiosity. They observe, wonder, and seek to understand by asking curious questions and listening. Curiosity is the choice state of open mindedness to explore options, possibilities, consider alternative points of view, foster innovation and creativity, and discover new solutions.

Leaders don't have to judge, diagnose, or "figure out" anyone. Leaders are aware and curious, noticing shifts in actions and behaviors in themselves and others, and ask "what's driving the behavior"? When they notice someone's countenance has fallen, they ask curious questions. What's going on that has shifted their behavior? Has something happened recently in the workplace, or elsewhere? Are they exhausted, or burned out? Have they been adapting out of their strengths? Have they been poked in a core value or important belief? Have they been recognized recently? Are their current needs being met? What are they thinking, feeling, wanting right now? Curiosity can lead to healthy dialogue to connect, seek understanding, encourage, support, and assist.

Curiosity is openness and acknowledging that I don't know what I don't know – and that's ok.

The opposite of curiosity is certainty. An important distinction needs to be recognized between the difference of clarity and certainty. Clarity is not absolute certainty in knowing. When a leader thinks that they know everything, they're right. The instant a leader believes this is the instant they close themselves off to learning anything new.

Absolute certainty is an oxymoron. Certainty in knowing becomes fixed, legalistic thinking, with tunnel vision that narrows focus. It's like living life seeing through a straw, so much else is missed. With absolute certainty, leaders firm up positions. Beliefs and opinions become "darn right" adamant inflexible stances.

When someone speaks with certainty by expressing or declaring an adamant position, it doesn't always mean they are right. It just means they're confident. Certainty can result in leaders limiting themselves to absolute, polar opposite, "either/or" positions, when often "both/and" options exist. They can become closed to opportunities that may be present and may not be exploring innovative options and solutions.

It seems obvious to proclaim with certainty that the shortest distance between two points is a straight line. The most efficient distance between two points is not always so straightforward.

In *"first you have to row a little boat"*, Richard Bode says the most efficient way to tack a boat into the wind is to sail a zigzag course, and offers many other examples: "A runner on second must advance to third base before he can score, even though the fastest way home is a diagonal through the heart of the diamond over the pitcher's mound. The most direct route from the line of scrimmage to the end zone is straight ahead, but it's a rare touchdown that's made that way; there are too many would-be tacklers between the ball carrier and the goal."[1]

Being curious or certain are choices leaders make every day in navigating the ebbs and flows of their life journey. Inspirational leaders choose curiosity, with confidence and humility, knowing they don't know everything, and that's ok. With healthy curiosity and less certainty, leaders move forward with openness to seek, and receive, new learning, perspective, and growth.

---

[1] Richard Bode, "first you have to row a little boat", 1993, page 49.

Being Curious and Less Certain
Reflection Questions

Where in your life do you practice being curious?

Where do you have the most certainty in your life?

Content to Dwell

Do you have the patience to wait until your mud settles and the water is clear? Can you remain unmoving till the right action arises by itself?

Lao Tzu

With fast paced lives leaders seek shortcuts to problem solving and decision making. When running at an unrelenting pace, leaders are sometimes tempted to press, rush to judgment, or make impulsive, reactive calls.

Neuroscience research has shown that our brains crave certainty. When there is ambiguity or uncertainty, an error response alerts the brain to pay attention, lights up the amygdale and arouses "fight or flight" in our limbic system.

Sometimes leaders need to slow down, even stop to turn off that striving, driving machine, and deeply listen. With silence and solitude time for deep listening, clarity comes.

Being content to dwell is a practice to trust and believe a course direction and solution will emerge.

Being content to dwell requires deep listening, a practice that opens us to receive fresh insights, face new challenges, remain calm under pressure with greater patience, see new possibilities, discover new solutions, think deeper and respond with greater innovation and creativity.

In *"Soul Keeping: Caring for the Most Important Part of You"*, author John Ortberg describes how leaders learn and grow during life challenges:

> *"What do we do in the dark night?*
>
> *We do nothing. We wait. We remember that we are not God.*
> *We hold on. We ask for help. We do less. We resign from things, we rest more, we stop going to church, we ask somebody else to pray because we can't.*
> *We let go of our need to hurry through it.*
>
> *You can't run in the dark."*[2]

---

[2] John Ortberg, "Soul Keeping: Caring for The Most Important Part of You", pg. 183.

At the beginning of a new year there are some days on the calendar where leaders can reasonably predict what they'll be doing or where they expect to be. No one can possibly foresee all that lies ahead. No matter how carefully planned, reality never really conforms well to the plan.

Being content to dwell in the midst of uncertainty and change is hard work. Not knowing the outcome can be unsettling and stressful in a season of navigating change and transition. It is tempting to press or try and brute force a solution even when one isn't readily available or visible. The automatic default mode is to continue hard charging and running the rat race.

Storms will come. Why lead with fear? Leaders can choose to face uncertainty. Especially in stressful times of change, being content to dwell helps leaders grow and strengthen emotional and situational awareness. Being content can strengthen and improve interactions with contentious people, vs. reacting and being contentious ourselves, which results in both parties mired in the slop.

Content to Dwell
Reflection Questions

Where, when, and how do you practice being content to dwell, with deep listening, trusting, and allowing your inner knowing to emerge?

How have you responded in navigating seasons of change and transition?

How have you responded encountering unplanned forks in the road?

How have you responded facing critical decisions?

Why Change is Hard

Though I do not believe that a plant will spring up
where no seed has been, I have great faith in a seed . . .
Convince me that you have a seed there,
and I am prepared to expect wonders.

Henry David Thoreau

Many habits and behaviors have been ingrained a long time. Conditioning is an automatic process where patterns of behavior and habit systems are set up in the brain in response to a stimulus that is repeated in our lives. When learning is productive, this is helpful. When learning is destructive, this is harmful.

Why is change such a challenge in the brain? Neuroscience research shows change requires several elements, including a) holding on to new information in our short-term working memory (that consumes lots of energy resources), b) a reduction of conflict with old information, c) time to allow new information to be registered and consolidated, and d) time for new information to be converted into an easy access form (like a compressed software file) that can be used with less energy. We need all of this to effect change, as opposed to just recalling the old habits that have already been consolidated in easy to retrieve form.

To break habit patterns, new brain circuits need to be formed that are stronger than the old ones. To change behavior, a new road is cut, vs. staying in the same ruts traveled. What is focused on creates connections, and paying attention will deepen the wiring. Attention changes the brain.

Leaders need to <u>see</u> the change (set attention),
<u>want</u> it (set intention),
and <u>believe</u> it can happen.

To clarify what is wanted requires one to go deeper than the head and cognitive thinking. Emotional connection with new desired choices drives *intention* and facilitates action.

One reason most New Year resolutions fail to stick is that we are trying to move straight from thinking (attention) to action, without having clarity of or sufficient want (intention). For example, when merely thinking about losing weight and going straight to action, without sufficient internal want and motivation for change. It is little surprise that we soon revert to our comfort zones, grabbing the chips and dip while watching bowl games.

What "want" looks like can be observed in the workplace. When people have clarity and motivation ("I want to take time off, to vacation, travel, celebrating the holidays . . .)", this internal desire provokes stressors that also serve as fuel for taking positive forward action.

With clarity of intention, people focus on whatever it takes to clear the decks and create space for manifesting what they want and realizing their desire.

Knowing what "want" looks like in December or summer vacation time enables leaders to clarify their intention and identify what they want at *any* time or season, and direct their energy to pursue their goals, hopes, and dreams.

Leaders may see the change, and want it, but there is one more critical variable that will facilitate and accelerate positive change. Leaders need to *believe* the desired change can happen. Whether you think you can, or you think you can't, you're likely to be right. Leaders may see and want hyper-growth forecasts that call for the business to triple in a year. But if they do not believe it can happen, it won't. Leaders must acknowledge, and resist, their internal voices of cynicism and skepticism.

For positive change to happen, leaders need to *see* the desired change (attention), *want* it (intention), and *believe* it can happen.

Why Change is Hard
Reflection Questions

What helps you clarify what you want, and drive your intention and desire for positive change?

What change do you *see (attention)*, and *want (intention)*, both short and longer term?

What do you need to truly believe the desired change can happen?

Seeing Light in Others

Building a Campfire

The sparks of the spirit cannot be kept from spreading, breaking through to each other. Like recognizes and is gathered to like in a manner none can explain.

Aleksandr Solzhenitsyn

How do you lead individuals and teams in the workplace? How do you grow leadership, build high performing teams, and create healthy cultures where people collaborate on a shared mission and flourish?

An executive leadership team of a global firm wanted to build on positive momentum and success they had experienced in the form of rapid revenue growth and profitability results. Their goals for the coming year were to have a common framework to strengthen relationships, inspire commitment, accelerate leadership growth, and foster healthy collaboration within a supportive organizational culture.

I was invited to join the team in the kickoff meeting of the new fiscal year to share a current topic on leadership and host a conversation to jump start the year.

No room is too small for the important work
of growing leaders. We create a spark
by meeting people right where they are,
fan the flame, and build a campfire.
Then, we build another campfire,
and another . . . until we have light!

Have you ever seen leaders and teams like this before? How would you meet a team right where they are, where would you start if you were invited to share a leadership topic and offer some general guidelines to help the team? How do you "build a campfire" and begin conversations about leadership in the workplace?

As soon as I entered the room, I could tell everyone was excited by the positive results, and I could also tell they were exhausted by the effort they had just expended to hit the finish line with a strong closing kick. It was just two days into the new fiscal year, the middle of the work week, and already they were turning the corner, discussing how they were going to top that effort, grow another X% and make their plan. They were ready to dive right back onto the hamster wheel and keep running.

When asked to step forward and share my presentation, I sensed an opportunity in the moment. I asked the leaders to indulge me for one to two minutes, and just for the moment sit in their chairs, and notice. They could close their eyes if they wished. I asked them to slow life down and soak in what success feels like.

I asked them to reflect on lives that they impacted in the past year. I started at a high level, consider the firm overall. Then, reflect on the lives in each of their respective offices, their peers and colleagues, employees they led, and their families. Next, consider clients and customers they helped. Appreciate the growth and great work accomplished working with each other as a team. Acknowledge their own personal contributions, and their families.

Simply altering pace by slowing down for a few moments created space to acknowledge success and express appreciation for each other for their collaboration and positive impact on the company culture. They were eager and open to tap into their curiosity for continuous learning and growth.

Sharing current topics is an incredible opportunity to connect with individual leaders and teams. Leaders are interested in learning new concepts, but only when translated with a "so what" connection and relevant application to how it fits into their world. Executive coaches can be eyes and ears on the ground for leaders who often are too busy to read an abundance of leadership books. With awareness of their interests, we can scan the marketplace, identify relevant resources, and help them connect the dots to their current roles and goals.

Meeting leaders and teams, right where they are, coaches ask curious questions to understand current context. What are their goals and professional aspirations?

Are they currently growing, plateauing, stagnant, declining, or struggling for survival? What are their challenges?

Serving as a sounding board, I listen to enable deeper thinking. I often hold up a mirror to enable the leader to clarify and affirm what's most important to them. Serving as a thinking partner, I meet them with research and success based perspectives from observations and lessons learned from thousands of leaders. I share tools and resources without attachment, the client chooses to use what fits best for themselves. Serving as an accountability partner, I challenge them to declare next action steps that will move them toward their goals.

Building a Campfire
Reflection Questions

What is your point of entry for meeting leaders, teams, and organizations right where they are? How to you create a spark and "build a campfire" that ignites a starting point for a healthy conversation for growing leaders and teams?

If you were asked to share a leadership topic, where would you start?

What are the leader's, and team, current goals and professional aspirations?

What are their current challenges and growing edge?

Recognizing Light in Others

If people aren't aware of their genius, they are not in position to deliberately utilize it. By telling people what you see, you can raise their awareness and confidence, allowing them to provide their capability more fully.[3]

Liz Wiseman

Leaders set the example and tone for the culture where they work and live. Leaders set vision, chart a compelling course for the future, align teams, inspire commitment, and empower others around them to act. Their actions and behaviors speak louder than what they say.

The impact leaders have on others is substantial. With keen eyes focused and their finely honed problem solving skills, it is tempting to see problems in people too. Failing to know, acknowledge, and nurture their hopes and aspirational dreams, or provide encouragement and support when it is helpful, leads to poor morale, disengagement, and high turnover. When people are managed and treated like they are computers with problems to be fixed, they too will burn out. The leader can ignite a spark, dampen, or snuff out the fire of enthusiasm.

---

[3] Liz Wiseman, "*Multipliers, Revised and Updated: How the Best Leaders Make Everyone Smarter*"

French mathematician Blaise Pascal has simple, profound words of encouragement for leaders: *"I bring you the gift of these four words: I believe in you."*

When people know you care about them, and believe in them, they'll take a hill for you. And the next hill, and the hill thereafter.

What are the professional career aspirations, hopes and dreams of the people who work for you? What are their next steps for forward growth? How can you feed this and accelerate their development?

Seeing light in others is looking past the protective armor and heavy baggage to see the rose within each person. It engages the whole portfolio of emotional intelligence competencies. Leaders who see light in others affirm them, assume noble intent, and give the benefit of the doubt.

When crossing paths with a colleague and casually asking them "How's it going?" how do you typically respond when they reply "Great"? In the busyness and rapid pace of a work day, do you usually just accept that reply, check the box, keep chugging along, and continue passing right by?

Great leaders know effective two-way communication is going beyond "Great". It's checking in with genuine interest, asking the next curious question. Knowing when, and how, to communicate. Great leaders are respectful and discerning, knowing some want frequent touch points, others prefer more space. Is now an appropriate time?

Words of encouragement are contagious. Healthy corporate cultures are created and sustained when people are encouraged to lead with their strengths and not their fears. Great leaders look for light in others, notice excellence, and seek to catch people doing good work. They check in to acknowledge what's working well, provide constructive guidance on what's not. They communicate to broaden and build upon positive behaviors and actions.

Leaders encourage people to go for it! They nudge them out of their comfort zone nests, urge them to stretch their boundaries, take steps into new arenas, and fly!

Recognizing Light in Others
Reflection Questions

What are the career aspirations, hopes and dreams of people who work for you?

What are their individual strengths? Their core values?

What do they love to do? How do they like to be recognized?

What are their proudest and most fulfilling accomplishments?

What are the next steps for their forward growth? How can you feed this and accelerate their development?

Being an Outlier is Your Contribution

Be yourself. The world worships the original.

Ingrid Bergman

My family relocated often as my dad transferred sales and marketing roles and climbed the corporate ladder. I was born in Bartlesville, Oklahoma, moved to Houston, Texas, then to Baton Rouge, Louisiana, and then migrated to a little town community in Canton, Connecticut, all before starting kindergarten. We moved to a rural community town of Hackettstown, New Jersey in the middle of fifth grade. Next, we moved across country to Los Angeles to the suburb of Inglewood, California in eighth grade. After that, my dad bought his own distributorship business that took the family to San Diego in the middle of ninth grade.

From kindergarten to high school, I walked into seven different schools in a variety of disparate locations and communities. Every time, it was starting over. Knowing no one, I felt like an outlier. The feeling only intensified as I grew older, with hardened tight cliques formed by classmates who had grown up together.

I learned to adapt to new environments and find my way, eventually meeting new friends who invited me into their circle.

There are many places we can find ourselves in the minority by gender, race, culture, status, faith, and age differences, to name only a few. I've had many experiences in the workplace where I've been the only one of "me" in the room (or severely outnumbered in proportion to the majority). I've been in rooms of hundreds of professional women with only a relative handful of men. I've been the only finance professional in a sea of sales, marketing, and HR leaders. I've been the oldest student by over twenty years among peers in the classroom.

At the beginning of a three day workshop with a group of thirty participants, as we were going around the room introducing ourselves, every individual shared their impressive backgrounds in counseling, human resources, and organizational development. I discovered myself once again as an outlier, in a room where I was the only one with business leadership and operations experience and coming from the world of finance. At the end of a long first day I left the session feeling like I didn't fit the group. It was going to be a very long three days.

I faced a choice as to how I would participate for the remainder of the workshop. I could either withdraw and sit passively as an outsider, and defer to the collective group. Alternatively, I could choose to be present, continue participating and get what I could from the sessions. I also recognized an opportunity as well. As an outlier, seeing the world a little differently from the rest, I could offer and share alternative perspectives and points of view. Being an outlier wasn't my *problem*. It was my *differentiator*, and if others were receptive, my *contribution* to the room.

Being an outlier is not your problem.
It's your <u>contribution.</u>

In *"Outliers: The Story of Success"*, Malcom Gladwell asserts "Outliers are those who have been given opportunities, and who have had the strength and presence of mind to seize them."[4] There is a difference between fitting in and belonging. Fitting in is adapting to group norms, often conceding what makes us unique, yielding to the consensus or withholding our input. Belonging is being all in, standing in our authenticity, bringing our whole selves and contributing our strengths.

A desire for belonging often comes at the expense of surrendering to follow others. Some withhold contributing or expressing alternative points of view that run counter to the leader or collective herd. However, being a passive team player may not be valued, recognized, or respected. When someone's voice is not heard, or people are unwilling to speak truth to power with confidence, they may be invisible in the crowd. Like a pawn in a chess game, they may be manipulated, taken advantage of, walked over, or rejected anyway.

---

[4] Malcolm Gladwell, *"Outliers: The Story of Success"*, 2011.

One of my core values is loving others in our differences. People do not all have to be the same. Whenever circumstances are reversed and I find myself in the majority, I seek to invite and welcome everyone into the room and encourage their contributions and perspectives.

People hold back when the environment is not deemed safe. When the room is open, people welcome differences. Learning and growth is enhanced and accelerated when individuals and collective groups choose to participate and share among each other.

Being an Outlier is Your Contribution
Reflection Questions

When have you experienced being an outlier?

How have you chosen to respond when you've experienced being an outlier either as an individual or significant minority in proportion to the group?

When have you experienced being an outlier as an opportunity to make a contribution to the group (instead of a problem)?

Who Do You Follow

on the Road Less Traveled?

When you have ceased to be afraid of threats and are not chasing after rewards – you become the most dangerous character in the owl-like view of the bosses. Because . . . what hold do they have on you?

Aleksandr Solzhenitsyn

People follow the direction of leaders much of their lives. Trust is placed in parents, teachers, coaches, mentors, and guides who provide wisdom and show the way forward. Soon after they're born, birds are encouraged to venture out of their comfort zone nest, to fly on their own and explore the world. Unless people too learn to spread their wings and fly themselves, relying on others can become unhealthy dependency or constrain them from becoming their best. Many resign and settle into designated places within family hierarchies, pecking orders, school cliques, and positional power in organizational structures.

There have been several times in my career where people have told me explicitly that I could not do what I was attempting to do.

Early in my career, I was looking to use my financial skills and track record in financial services and consulting to seek opportunities to work inside a manufacturing and distribution firm. A recruiter told me I couldn't. She emphatically stated, "You're a high priced banker, you'll always be a high priced banker." A few months later, she reconnected with me in my role leading treasury operations for a $500 million company.

A career counselor told me to stop chasing rainbows: "Why don't you give up and go back to doing mergers and acquisitions?" Several recruiters have acknowledged to me they are not creative when it comes to filling open positions. History is the best predictor of the future. If one wishes to detour off of the same logical conventional path (or treadmill) and explore new directions, they've been on for years they'll fall off the grid.

Many people are ready and willing to tell people how to run their lives. Most may be well intentioned, but don't know any options other than dispensing wisdom, advice, and unsolicited opinions. Throughout my career, I've encountered individuals acting "better than", protecting their turf and barriers to entry. Some individuals have short-sighted opinions and are quick to identify the problem ("You don't have experience"). Others rush to judgment ("You can't), or freely dispense their wisdom by telling you how to fix your life ("Give up!). Naysayer critics should not have power to discourage or deter from exploring new paths.

Transformational change is not for the faint of heart. However, shifting careers, moving to new industries, or functional areas of expertise can be done.

The ability for healthy discernment is paramount. Clarify what you want, then declare it and step out in faith. Reach out and ask for help. Be open to receive input. Use discernment for guidance and grit to stay the course through the ebbs and flows. Nurture resilience in order to get back up from setbacks and falls and keep going.

I am grateful to have met many inspirational leaders and mentors who listened and provided encouragement, support, were willing to take a risk, give me a chance, and believed in me.

A seasoned career counselor listened to my story, asked curious questions about my professional accomplishments and desire for helping others and assessed, "You're not a career counselor. You're an executive coach!"

An Organizational PhD and leadership consultant, recognizing the opportunity to collaborate and leverage strengths for great synergy, invited me to facilitate leadership development workshops for a global technology client and coach high performing leaders growing emotional intelligence.

A Chief Human Resource Officer counseled me, "Don't compete with OD people on their terms. Just keep talking with me about my business. You'll be great!"

Who do you follow on the road less traveled?
Who are inspirational leaders who exemplify
courage and show the way for you?

Belonging to a group or organization does not mean blind submission to another, or capitulation to the collective herd. When the default is to follow others, leadership is conceded to someone who steps into the void and assumes the mantle of leader of the pack. Often this is the loudest, most assertive or aggressive voice. This is a risky strategy, as success depends on another person's agenda. One can only hope the leader deferred to shares similar values and ethical standards.

Blindly following others is being a passenger in someone else's car, going along for the ride wherever they'll take you. It's time spent living someone else's dream at the expense of pursuing your own.

Who Do You Follow on the Road Less Traveled?
Reflection Questions

Who are inspirational examples of leaders who show you what courage looks like?

Who do you follow on the road less traveled? When navigating change, engaging uncertainty, or exploring uncharted pathways, are there leaders who show the way for you?

How do you check in with what your heart and gut are telling you?

A Team Player is not a Pushover

An ideal team player is humble, hungry, and smart.[5]

Patrick Lencioni

Many professionals excel at conducting financial and other business transactions. Private equity investors, venture capitalists, investment bankers, mergers and acquisition specialists, and litigators are among many who develop highly specialized expertise, structure complex deals, and fight hard negotiating on behalf of their constituent stakeholders. They seek strategic and tactical opportunities to optimize returns on investment by leveraging advantages and exploiting disadvantages of the other side. When operating in an adversarial environment, negotiation can become a way of life.

I've worked with many leaders and service providers who describe themselves as being team players. They work tirelessly with dedicated commitment in pursuit of their firm or their client's goals. They're aligned with the group consensus, and generally prefer not to stand out from the crowd or be seen as rocking the boat.

---

[5] Patrick Lencioni, *"The Ideal Team Player: How to Recognize and Cultivate the Three Essential Virtues"*, 2016.

In his best-selling book *"The Ideal Team Player"*, Patrick Lencioni describes three virtues of an ideal team player:

1) Humble (with grounded confidence),
2) Hungry, (get stuff done, drive for results), and
3) Smart (emotional intelligence, the ability to be interpersonally appropriate and aware).

What makes an ideal team player is the required combination of all three virtues.

An overly compliant team player who is unwilling to push back can lose the respect of the client. If a team player enables the client to run over them, often they will.

If the client is late providing critical information required to complete the overall mission, one option a team player has is to step up, remain resolved and committed to the original plan while sacrificing every member on the team to cough up their work/life balance working days, weeks, and months of overtime and late evenings to make up lost time. Working everyone with no let up to physical exhaustion may succeed and get the job done in the short run, but end up with a trail of worn out bodies in the wake, and decrease retention when many quit.

There are times when a team player needs to take a firm stance and raise their hand, especially if they're in the team huddle and can see that the play being called won't work.

A cliché of finance is "he who has the gold makes the rules". If you're the employee or service provider, and I'm the employer or the client, who pays the bills, that translates to you work for me.

Sometimes a team player needs to clarify roles and expectations up front and throughout the engagement with the employer or client. It's not an "us vs. them" adversarial relationship. Rather it's "we're all in this together, working collaboratively toward a common goal".

Sometimes a team player needs to stand up for their team, to communicate the deadline will slip, or fees will increase, because of late negative surprises. Sometimes a team player may even need to splash water in the face of a bully to get their attention, and communicate it's not ok to mistreat or abuse members of the team.

A team player willing to stand up and push back, speaking truth to power with a clear business case often earns and retains the respect of the employer or client, particularly those used to working in an adversarial environments and negotiating as a way of life.

A Team Player is not a Pushover
Reflection Questions

What does being a team player mean to you?

When have you been at your best as a team player?

When have you had to take a firm stance as a team player communicating with an employer or client?

How do you earn and grow respect as a team player?

Who best models an "Ideal Team Player", someone who demonstrates the combination of Humble, Hungry, and Smart virtues?

Growing the Light Within

Success Leaves Clues

Successes leave footprints for future successes.[6]

Relly Nadler

Reflection is a powerful tool for discovery and clarification. Reflection reveals, liberates, and transforms. A lot happens when you take a step back to listen and look at your life. When you slow yourself down, you can see the journey you've taken and the process of transformation that has been going on throughout your life. Many answers to your most profound questions about your career and your life can be found a lot closer than you might realize.

***Every once in a while it's a good idea
to get out of the trees and look from
the forest perspective. Climb to the summit,
look over the landscape. See the path where
you've come, assess where you are, make sure
you're still heading the right direction,
and reset your path if you want to.***

---

[6] Reldan S. Nadler, Psy.D., "Leading with Emotional Intelligence: Hands-on Strategies for Building Confident and Collaborative Star Performers", 2011.

Look at your life experiences, scan significant summit points in your life and review choices you've made. Recognize important people you've met who have had significant impact in your life and career. Some new insights may jump out. Many common themes are often repeated at different stages throughout your career and your life.

The spadework of reflection can be liberating. For best results, be totally honest and open with yourself. Have a willingness to let go and not hold anything back.

The purpose of reflection is not to dwell on or get stuck in the past, but use your life and career experiences to your advantage in the present, to take positive steps toward the direction that gives you energy and joy. A more enlightened awareness of knowing who you are and where you've been enables you to stay focused on what matters most.

Success Leaves Clues
Reflection Questions

Reflect on your life journey. Draw a life map, with some of the ups and downs, peak and valley moments.

What are the most fulfilling "up" experiences and accomplishments in your life and career? Flesh out these experiences in some detail. What was the challenge, problem, or situation? What was your role, what action did you take? What was the result, and impact?

What skills do you notice yourself utilizing? Are these clues to some skills you want to continue using moving forward?

Adversity Lessons

*Nothing ever goes away until it has taught us
what we need to know.[7]*

Pema Chodron

How have you responded in difficult moments in your life? How quickly do you adapt and grow after a setback, fall, or disappointment?

**Reflection can give clarity of purpose
during difficult periods of navigating change
or career transitions where you may have time
and opportunity to figure things out.**

How have you overcome adversity in the past? Maybe it was through grit, perseverance, or tenacity. Maybe it was courage, optimism, some supportive mentors and encouraging friends. You still have these strengths now.

Our experiences shape and inform our core values and beliefs, reveal life lessons, form narrative stories that shape and change our world view.

---

[7] Pema Chodron, *"When Things Fall Apart: Heart Advice for Difficult Times"*, 1997.

How are these life lessons, world views, stories, and beliefs serving you now? Are they still enabling you in a positive way today? Perhaps there are some beliefs that are no longer serving you well, even limiting or holding you back in some way. Are some stories of the past defining you? Some beliefs can be useful in moving us through a difficult time, but not so applicable or even unhelpful other times.

Clarifying our life lessons, reflecting and getting our stories right builds resilience for facing future challenges and bouncing back from setbacks and disappointments that will arise. Recognizing we have faced adversity with courage before provides courage in the present.

Frank Sinatra boldly sings about resilience: *"I've been a puppet, a pauper, a pirate, a poet, a pawn and a king. I've been up and down and over and out, and I know one thing: Each time I find myself flat on my face, I pick myself up and get back in the race. That's life!"*[8]

With more enlightened awareness of life lessons from facing and overcoming adversity in the past, you can learn to accept yourself and your feelings. You can notice how you've responded to difficult situations before to be aware of any reactive triggers and more constructive responses in the present. With reflection you can clarify your life stories, reframe them, and write new endings. Whatever cannot be changed can be accepted. You can make healthy choices and adjustments going forward, and significantly reduce negative time spent engaged in certain problems.

---

[8] "That's Life", Dean Kay/Kelly L. Gordon, Universal Music Publishing Group

Adversity Lessons
Reflection Questions

How have you overcome adversity in the past? What do you do when circumstances go awry?

Describe some of your "down" life experiences, situations when you've had a setback, failure, or disappointment, endured under duress pressure, or adversity.

What strengths have helped you move through difficult and challenging times?

What life lessons did you learn from these experiences? How was your world view shaped, or changed? What beliefs emerged?

How are these life lessons, world views, stories, and beliefs serving you today? Are they still true? Are they enabling? Any limiting or holding you back?

Identify Blind Spots and

Derailing Behaviors

The absolute heart of loyalty is to value those people who tell you the truth, not just those people who tell you what you want to hear. In fact, you should value them most. Because they have paid you the compliment of leveling with you and assuming you can handle it.

Pat Summitt

How do leaders discover blind spots and derailing behaviors? Becoming aware of our flaws and deficiencies can sometimes feel like awakening in a dark tunnel. If we find ourselves there, how do we get out?

This was the challenge faced by a leader of a global firm. The Chief Human Resources Officer approached me to work with an operations leader to improve communication and peer relationships. A 360 survey from his colleagues had revealed some negative feedback and significant derailing behaviors he needed to eliminate. The leader was a problem-solving task manager with a heavy command and control style. Hard driving his team, he often left people behind as he bulldozed down the path, executing his plan.

I met with the leader to discuss the coaching process and assess his readiness and fit for working together. The leader reluctantly accepted the offer for coaching, but dismissed the 360 feedback as flawed data. He believed he had merely picked the wrong people for the survey!

We began our engagement by conducting a variety of self-assessments that identified and confirmed many clear strengths. The leader was skilled at getting things done, navigating change, crisis management, and problem solving. He could consolidate and close plants on time and under budget, and had a proven track record of success, consistently doing so for twenty years. He handled stress well, stayed calm and persevered. He thrived working under intense pressure. He was also optimistic, enjoyed his work and found meaning in it.

However, the leader's self-assessments also confirmed the negative data that surfaced in the 360 feedback. The self-assessments revealed the leader had close to zero emotional self-awareness. This self-indictment served as a big splash of water that awakened the leader's consciousness. The leader shared, "I don't know how to talk to people." Heightened awareness stirred a motivation for positive change and opened his channel of curiosity.

The leader was not an emotionless, stoic rock. He had feelings and thoughts like all of us. However, he only opened himself up and shared when people were being shepherded out the door. As a result, others perceived him as insincere and transactional.

Emotional self-awareness is the catalyst,
the domino that tips all other emotional
intelligence leadership competencies,
and opens a channel for growth.

With raised awareness, motivation to change, curiosity to learn, and courage to engage, the leader began by reflecting on the data received. He distilled key takeaway actions, and crafted a development plan for growth. His plan had four expressed goals: 1) growing emotional self-awareness by being more open to expressing positive emotions to enable others to better know and understand him, 2) growing situational awareness through his interactions, 3) growing empathy and listening skills, and 4) developing a more strategic focus on the bigger picture balanced with the granular analytical details.

All of these goals had high degrees of difficulty! One of the first steps in growing self-awareness was reflecting upon and clarifying his core values, then declaring his personal intentional commitment to his development plan. The leader shared his plan with his leader for buy-in and support. One of the most significant behaviors in building trust in teams is asking for help. The leader's next steps were to courageously approach each of the participants in the original 360 survey. He thanked them for their collective feedback, shared his development plan response, and invited them to partner with him as he stretched out of his comfort zone. He welcomed their participation and also shared that he was working with an executive coach.

Soon after an urgent email arrived calling a team together on another complex crisis project. Instead of having months to complete in a reasonable time frame, the team was given only a few weeks to come up with solutions.

This was a real life opportunity to implement his development plan. When the team assembled for its initial meeting, the leader began by taking a few moments up front to share his reactions. The leader shared with the team that he felt stressed when he received the email and felt stressed by the challenge ahead. He checked in with others to see how they were feeling too. He shared the initial game plan for moving forward, and invited others to share their ideas. Throughout this time he would also be working on his development plan. He asked for support from his team members while offering it for them.

The leader learned that opening up to others was not simply dumping angst on people. He learned there is power in expressing thoughts and feelings and being willing to share vision, values, goals, hopes and dreams.

Getting things started by turning in the direction of forward growth had positive, rippling effects for both the leader and the company. The leader's clarity of goals, courageousness in asking for help, and stepping out of his comfort zone, enabled perceptions of him to change. These shifting behaviors of the leader also served as inspiration for the leader's boss. He approached me at the end of the formal coaching engagement asking for executive coaching support to develop his own plan for forward growth.

Identify Blind Spots and Derailing Behaviors
Reflection Questions

How do you grow your emotional self-awareness?

What are your non-negotiable core values?

What helps you grow your *situational* awareness?

How often do you ask for help from others?

What are your next steps for professional growth and development as a leader?

Notice Your Pace

You must ruthlessly eliminate hurry from your life.[9]

Dallas Willard

Are you aware, and intentional, of your current pace? Are you racing to complete an important task today? Sprinting with a closing kick to a finish line milestone accomplishment? Running a longer distance marathon? Striving to get up to speed, or hitting the ground running on a new project? Scurrying to clear the decks and head off for vacation? Why are you running?

Many leaders are "Type A" personalities wired to be highly proactive throughout the workday. They are driven to get lots of tasks done, often under tight deadlines and time constraints. A high power executive once shared he didn't even know how to slow down. He was always running 120 miles an hour!

Running at a rapid, unrelenting pace can become operating on automatic. Over time, business becomes "busy-ness" toil moving from one task to another all day.

---

[9] John Ortberg, *"Soul Keeping: Caring for the Most Important Part of You"*, 2014.

Hard charging leaders can be so immersed in their work intensity that they have little awareness as to how intimidating they're perceived by others as they charge down the hallway. They may lose perspective and miss significant learning and growth opportunities.

Before leaders can receive, they need to turn off that hard striving, driving machine. Resist the routine temptation to keep running, by intentionally pausing to disrupt the flow of a breakneck pace. Just noticing and altering cadence can get us off automatic and helps us see with greater clarity.

Notice your current pace and cadence.
Do they match the race you're running?
Why are you running?

Sometimes slowing down, even a little, helps. This is true even when there is a mountain of tasks awaiting our attention. Drivers have a lot more operational control when they lighten their foot off the accelerator from 120 to 80 mph, even more at 60 mph. Slowing down sometimes positions leaders to receive fresh thinking, assimilate new learning, pause to survey the big picture direction, and consider course correction adjustments.

Eddie Cantor once said, "Slow down and enjoy life. It's not only the scenery you miss by going too fast – you also miss the sense of where you're going and why."

In his book "*Stopping – How to Be Still When You Have To Keep Going*" Dr. David Kundtz says "Stopping brings you awake and aware of the present moment. But it also helps you bring together the threads of your history, of your stories. It helps you to remember who you are, where you come from, where you are going, and where you want to go; to remember your original goals, ideals, and dreams; and to remember why you started doing what you do so that you can see if that's still what you want to do. Even if you have no clear answers for many of the big questions of life, it is vital to continue to remember what your questions are. Losing your questions is truly losing your way."[10]

Run your own race and set your own pace. It's ok to alter cadence to meet challenges and circumstances. There are times when it's best to sprint, other times to jog, walk, and sit. Noticing pace heightens awareness, enabling leaders to be open to receive, learn and grow. They are in a better position to evaluate priorities and progress, make adjustments, and appreciate what they're doing, and why.

---

[10] "*Stopping – How to Be Still When You Have to Keep Going*", Dr. David Kundtz, Conari Press, 1998, p45.

Notice Your Pace
Reflection Questions

Notice your pace for the next week. Is it fast (too fast?), or slow (too slow?)?   Are you running a sprint, or a marathon? Why are you running?

When and how does your pace shift from time to time?

How are you positioned to receive and assimilate fresh thinking and new learning?

Watch Your Self-Talk

What can be done about the weather in my head?

Donald Fagen

Neuroscience research says there are two circuits in the brain that are completely separate from each other. A Narrative circuit channels our thinking about the past and future. It focuses on concepts and stories. A Direct Experience circuit senses incoming data about the present. These two circuits are anti-correlated. When one circuit is on, the other is turned off. Throughout the day most people talk to themselves in the narrative circuit. Several hours every day are engaged in thinking about something that has happened in the past, or about something that could happen in the future.

French philosopher Michel de Montaigne once said, "My life has been filled with terrible misfortune, most of which never happened." We can concoct our own bait and trigger ourselves by making up narrative stories. By reading more into an email communication and misinterpreting intentions of the sender. Seeing someone react to something we said or did, then rushing to judgment, quickly voting, and ascribing motivations to others. When not hearing from someone, after a while we make up a story and start to believe they don't care about us.

It is normal business practice to forecast and plan for best, realistic, and worst case scenarios. However, life has an infinite number of possibilities. Most are unforeseen and can't possibly be orchestrated in advance. We have no idea who we'll meet on the path ahead, what ideas and insights will be discovered, or what new vistas will be encountered just further down the road.

Negative self-talk clouds thinking and blocks out light. Fears and concerns can become a self-fulfilling prophecy when we doubt and speak to ourselves with debilitating shame language ("You're not good enough" and "Who do you think you are?"), worrying and dwelling on worst case scenarios. We head towards where we aim our focus, and attract what we seek.

Studies have shown that Ferrari drivers crash into telephone poles at a higher proportion than other drivers. If so, what are some reasons why this would happen? Maybe they're driving too fast. Maybe they're going so fast they lose control. Even so, why do they hit the pole? Because it's where they're looking. Then what is a solution, when you find yourself going too fast and out of control? Don't look at the pole!

Studies have shown people are quick to vote with a negative bias too. One Monday morning an executive leader in transition shared with a networking support group, "I got an email with some bad news this morning. I learned I didn't make the cut, and I'm out of the running for the position I wanted. Well, today is shot!"

It was *9am* in the morning. He was understandably disappointed. However, there was a whole lot of daylight left. There was opportunity to reset, recover and reclaim a victory or two, or at least make it a better day. Deciding quickly shuts off being open to opportunities for receiving new insights and learning.

Your life is as good as your thoughts make it. Goethe once said, "I have come to the frightening conclusion that I am the decisive element. It is my personal approach that creates the climate. It is my daily mood that makes the weather." Neuroscience and mindfulness research indicates thoughts last about 90 seconds, and can drift away like a bird or a cloud in the sky, unless they are fed.

When we find ourselves ruminating on a new negative thought, it's time to stop, and ask ourselves a question. Will I allow this to become a new mantra in my head, or choose to stop feeding it and let it drift away? Whenever we are able to catch ourselves in self-talk narratives, we can stop ruminating in an endless loop mantra playing over and over in our head. We can turn the light back on instantly by shifting focus to the present.

Every time we notice negative self-talk, stop, redirect and shift focus to the present, we are building resilience, strengthening our ability to bounce back from setbacks and disappointments.

Redirecting focus to the present raises our awareness. We can choose to lighten up on ourselves, be less self-critical and have more self-compassion. We can choose to remember people who have set positive examples. We can celebrate and honor them in the present for their contribution to our life. We can surround ourselves with positive people, inspirational affirmations, listen to music, or explore sights, sounds, tastes and other senses that enrich and bring joy.

There are two important victories with this practice. The first victory is noticing and stopping negative talk. The second victory is redirecting focus to the present. Choosing to see what the day has right in front of us, hearing birds singing, smelling coffee, the roses, (or soap in the shower!)

Even a very small change in focus each day is an opportunity for significantly enhancing our quality of life. Eliminating just ten minutes of negative self-chatter each day results in over an hour a week in time savings with more positive time in the present. Over a year, an additional hour of being present each week is a 52 hour vacation. With less distractions and improved focus, what could you do with ten minutes of extra time each day?

There are choices that can set the course of life experience. One can choose to live life worrying about one problem, solving it, then worrying about the next one. Or, alternatively, choose to move from one success to the next success, or from one joy to the next. We can choose to ruminate – or celebrate!

Watch Your Self-Talk
Reflection Questions

For the next week, notice your self-talk. When you catch yourself in a narrative story, thinking about the past or future, shift focus to the present.

Notice your breath in the moment. Activate at least one of your five senses. Pause to notice (the view, sights and activity around you), listen (music, laughter, birds chirping), smell (the roses, the coffee, soap, a bakery), taste (slow down to savor your food), and touch.

If you find yourself ruminating over anything, stop, notice and ask: Will I allow this to become a new mantra in my head, or choose to stop feeding it?

With less distractions and improved focus, what could you do with ten minutes of extra time each day?

Know Your Triggers

You may not control all the events that happen to you, but you can decide not to be reduced by them.

Maya Angelou

A high potential leader described exasperation at spending hours of time reacting to a slew of urgent, often conflicting demands from executive management. Inefficient administrative tasks were consuming and distracting her focus from more the productive activity of generating revenue and profit. Frustration was especially heightened when no one was willing to make decisions at the upper levels. Constructive suggestions for improvement were summarily blown off.

When her voice was not heard or valued, she recoiled internally and shut down. She didn't lash out or visibly react, but felt diminished and angry for several days. After suffering through another recent incident, she shared "I wish I was conscious enough of these kinds of triggering issues to be able to calmly evaluate the situation in front of me and respond better."

We are containers for thinking and feeling, and both drive behaviors. When emotionally triggered, feelings increase proportionally, and compromise clear thinking. When triggered, there is an instant reaction that is typically a version of fight, flight or freeze. Situations can trigger people to lash out, jump into fix it mode, escalate, criticize or blame others (fight). Alternatively, people can become defensive, withdraw, shut down, or isolate themselves (flight). Some get stuck, spend hours, days, or longer ruminating in a loop of unproductive self-talk (freeze).

Aristotle said, "Anybody can become angry. That is easy. But to be angry with the right person, and to the right degree, and at the right time, and for the right purpose, and in the right way, that is not within everyone's power, and is not easy." Ancient wisdom that holds well in today's light.

What are emotional triggers? Can we identify when "bait" is tossed, or the "buttons" are pushed by others, when we give power away to someone or something?

We can't prevent triggering events,
but we can grow to reduce our reactivity.
We can lower the <u>intensity</u>, <u>frequency</u>,
and <u>duration</u> of how we respond to them.

Think of a recent conflict or negative situation, something that really "pushed your emotional buttons", or really hurt or upset you. How did it make you feel?

What are some options to help manage emotions when triggered? Relly Nadler's Emotional Audit[11] tool asks five simple, strategic questions that can help change the focus when a person is emotionally triggered:

What am I thinking right now?
What am I feeling right now?
What do I want right now?
How am I getting in my own way (holding me back)?
What do I want to do now (what is my next step)?

Using the Emotional Audit as a frequent check, numerous times a day even before a hijack event, builds self-awareness, self-management, and resilience.

When triggered, things don't make sense. However, one can refocus activity away from the brain's limbic system (fight, flight, or freeze) to other areas of the brain in order to gain more cognitive control. Leaders can learn to take full ownership of their feelings, actions, and behaviors. They create space, pause to notice, and reflect. Leaders can choose to respond and not react. They identify what they can control and let go what they can't.

The goal is to identify, understand, and manage emotions first. Be able to respond, not react, and not give power away to anyone to hijack our life. When aware of our emotional triggers, we're more resilient and present, less likely to give power away.

---

[11] *Leading with Emotional Intelligence* Reldan S. Nadler, Psy.D., 2011, pages 96-97.

Know Your Triggers
Reflection Questions

Think of a recent conflict or negative situation that really hurt or upset you. How did it make you feel? How did you react in the moment? (Fight? Flight? Freeze?)

What was the triggering event? What "buttons" were pushed? Has a core value been poked? Have you taken "bait" and given power to anyone to hijack your life?

Has lightness and ease been compromised for hyper-seriousness and intense? Are you keeping the BIG PICTURE in mind?

What is the story you're telling yourself? How much is fact vs. assumptions? Has communication been clear?

Is certainty a factor? Are people (including myself) digging in with adamant, inflexible positions? Are they right, or merely confident? How am I defending or explaining my position? Can I do this with calm, gentle persuasion?

I am excited to announce publication of my latest leadership book!

"Leading with Light" shares wisdom insights and lessons learned from inspirational leaders with reflections for application for greater clarity, building confidence, and more fulfillment in the workplace.

REQUEST: I ask your help! Write a review and post on Amazon.com.

What does it mean to lead with light?

There is light in each of us. When leaders grow self-awareness in knowing who they are and living their core values and strengths, light emerges from within and shines brightest. Light itself also illumines the path for leaders to grow situational awareness of where they are in the moment, set goals and chart compass direction, thereby opening up a channel of curiosity for learning, exploring, and discovery. Seeing light in others, leaders encourage and challenge others to shine their own lights and become their highest and best.

Working with thousands of leaders across all functional areas, from a wide variety of industries, from global companies to small businesses, I've seen what brings out the best in leaders. These are best practices and simple tools that will enable you to grow as a leader. You'll be fully seen as your brightest and most authentic self, courageous in exploring new vistas, pursuing goals with tenacity, and manifesting your vision to reality. You will build stronger relationships, grow resilience in navigating change, and learn and grow from setbacks and disappointments.

YOU are a beacon of light! Own it.

Is Rest a Value?

Learn from yesterday. Live for today.
Look to tomorrow. Rest this afternoon.

Snoopy

I've heard it said that for every day engaged in intensive activity or training, leaders need a day for recovery.

While my head registered this logically, my body had to weigh in to help me appreciate and integrate this sage wisdom the hard way. One year I facilitated several weekend intensive leadership retreats. Ending midday Sunday, I rested for the rest of the day. I was feeling fulfilled but wiped out from a highly impactful experience for participants. Then, it was right back to work Monday morning with a full slate of coaching sessions. By the time I took a well-earned break at the end of the year, I was exhausted. The immune system in my body was so depleted I caught a nasty case of the flu that sidelined me for weeks.

During busy season crunch times, leaders load up on work. They are often overwhelmed with hyper-activity and fast pace, racing to hit critical project milestones and completion deadlines. Limits are tested as our dedication and hard work ethic can become overused strengths and stretched beyond optimal points of productivity.

Bad habits, even well intentioned, can lead to physical breakdowns. I've encountered dozens of high potential leaders who have pushed themselves so far beyond their physical and emotional stress limits that they land in emergency rooms with health problems that wouldn't typically start showing in most people for another twenty years. Working too hard and too many hours every day, for many weeks, and months can be costly and come at inopportune times.

The Center for Disease and Control defines sleep debt as less than seven hours of sleep in a 24-hour period. As sleep debt accumulates, our work output is progressively deteriorating. This results in diminishing marginal returns for the work day. During a long work day, we wear ourselves down. There comes a point when leaders become less productive with each additional hour pushed later and later into the evening (and early morning).

Working long and late hours for weeks and months on complex mergers and acquisitions transactions, my colleagues had a saying that we often reminded ourselves: Anything interesting at 3pm in the afternoon wasn't that interesting at 3am in the morning.

Rest is a good idea. We know this logically in the head. Does rest rise to the level of being a core value for you?

When tired, worn out, and exhausted, negative things happen cognitively, physically, and emotionally. Tired leaders become more irritable and forgetful. With depleted energy and weakened immune systems, worn out and exhausted leaders become more stressed and reactive.

When running on fumes,
we're more likely to be fuming!

The benefits of rest and refreshment are many and obvious. Restoration and energy recharges enable clear thinking. Getting away from the tight focus on the problem for fresh perspective and finding more energy for identifying solutions. Sleeping on an important decision is great for discernment and next action steps.

Exercising, getting the blood flowing, getting away from the problem, clears the mind too. Resting the mind by playing a game of tennis in the midst of a busy season is client service. We can be more productive when we intentionally rest, refresh, and recharge. This is especially before beginning a closing kick finish where we want to be our strongest, clearest thinking, energized selves.

When rest is a value, we prioritize it. Limiting intake, screens and heavy concentration an hour before sleep helps calm and rest the mind. After heavy travel or intensive days, schedule a lighter day to help reset energy levels.

Is Rest a Value?
Reflection Questions

Does rest rise to the level of being a core value for you?

How do you prioritize rest, recovery, refresh, and recharge your batteries?

What time boundaries and commitments are for today?

How do you monitor your level of sleep? How do you recover sleep debt?

Do you set aside a day once a week for rest? What's stopping you?

Lightening the Load

Lighten Up for

Peak Performance

Rule #6: Don't take yourself so seriously!

Ben Zander

In *"The Art of Possibility"*[12], Benjamin Zander advises every leader to always remember Rule Number 6. This rule is very simple: Don't take yourself so seriously. When asked what the other rules are, he replies, "There aren't any."

It is a safe assumption that the vast majority of executive leadership jobs require a consistent, heavy dose of intensive thinking and concentration. Our brains have a working memory in the prefrontal cortex that is used for learning new activities. Our left brain processes critical thinking, problem solving, and other forms of highly focused attention. Both require a lot of energy to function optimally, and both fatigue easily.

---

[12] *"The Art of Possibility: Transforming Professional and Personal Life"*, Rosamund Stone Zander and Benjamin Zander, 2002, pg. 79.

Overuse for a prolonged period, like pushing the accelerator of a car and not taking the foot off the gas, will eventually take its toll physically, mentally, and emotionally. When brains are taxed with depleting energy resources, people get exhausted and distracted. Over-thinking can become an overused strength. Leaders become tightly focused on a problem, often stuck in "analysis paralysis" that hinders making clear decisions or taking action.

> *Lightening up backs off the intensity and seriousness, enabling us to operate less only from the head and contribute more from the heart.*

We can dial down the intensity and heat of the moment by lightening up. What are some options? For starters, neuroscience research has shown that even a few minutes of slowing down and quiet mindfulness each day helps increase attention and focus. It increases perception and generates more insights. It also improves resilience. Moreover, better self-regulation, the ability to be more in charge of attention, emotions, focus, impulses, and reactivity is the very heart of successful leadership.

Lighten Up for Peak Performance
Reflection Questions

Have you ever experienced being "over-serious" in yourself or with others? What does this look like?

Have you ever experienced "over-thinking"? What does this look like?

How can you lighten up the intensity, back off the accelerator, and take yourself a little less seriously from time to time?

Look in the mirror. Ask yourself, "Would I talk to me right now"? Can you pass the "mirror test"?

Loosen Up for

Peak Performance

Exercise gives you endorphins. Endorphins make you happy. Happy people just don't shoot their husbands. They just don't![13]

Elle Woods

Wouldn't this be a great world if insecurity and desperation made us more attractive? If "needy" were a turn-on? [14]

Aaron Altman

In addition to lightening up, one can optimize performance by loosening up too. One morning before beginning a second challenging day of an intensive workshop, a cohort participant asked me a simple question:

"What do you do to loosen up before entering the arena?"

---

[13] Reese Witherspoon, *"Legally Blonde"*, 2001, quotes imdb.com
[14] Albert Brooks, *"Broadcast News"*, 1987, quotes imdb.com

The "arena" is any place, event, situation, or conversation where you want to be courageous and show up your authentic best.

In the moment, I responded that I take some time to center myself. Breathing does help calm me and is a good practice recommendation for anyone. However, as I later paused to reflect on our conversation, I realized I had not actually answered the question she had asked. She had not asked me how I calmed myself. She asked what I did to loosen up. A subtle but important nuance distinction.

When we loosen up, we move. In *"The Gifts of Imperfection"*, social researcher and author Brené Brown describes guideposts for wholehearted living[15]. Activities that get people moving are laughter, song, and dance.

What helps you loosen up
before stepping into the arena?

What helps loosen me up before entering an arena, like stepping in front of the room to deliver an important presentation, or facilitating a workshop? Listening to high energy singalongs and positivity anthem songs that get me out of my head for a few moments and go with the flow.

How can you lessen intensity operating only from the head and bring more depth contribution from the heart?

---

[15] *"The Gifts of Imperfection: Let Go of Who You Think You're Supposed to Be and Embrace Who You Are; Your Guide to a Wholehearted Life"*, 2010, Brené Brown, Ph.D., L.M.S.W., pg. 117.

What makes you move? What are some anthem songs that energize, uplift and inspire? What makes you laugh?

Being open to spontaneous laughter whenever it arises can lighten any mood. Watching hilarious movies or shows can also do the trick. In *Legally Blonde* we benefit from the wisdom of intern lawyer Elle Woods. In *Broadcast News*, the musings of Aaron Altman. I laugh every time I see *Butch Cassidy and the Sundance Kid*, *The Big Lebowski*, or *Ghostbusters*. There are lots of options. *The Good Place, The Office, Parks and Recreation, Everybody Loves Raymond,* and *Scrubs* also work for me.

How can you play more, relax, loosen up to really enjoy being and engaging the present?

Loosen Up for Peak Performance
Reflection Questions

What do you do to loosen up before entering the arena (any place, event, situation, or important conversation) where you want to show up at your authentic best?

What are some anthem songs that inspire, energize, and uplift you?

What makes you laugh?

The Liberating Power

of Letting Go

*When we really delve into the reasons for why
we can't let something go, there are only two:
an attachment to the past or a fear of the future.*[16]

Marie Kondo

Neuroscientists describe the brain's negativity bias that states we tend to dwell more on negative feedback and dismiss the positive. Sensitivity to one negative comment can outweigh over a dozen positives. Negative people can push buttons and throw us off our game.

People hold grudges, resentments, past hurts and regrets. Holding on to these negative emotions is like pushing beach balls under water and trying to swim. Storing requires energy, tightens, and makes us bitter. There may be some limiting beliefs that once served us well, but now may be holding us back and keeping us from being our best.

---

[16] Marie Kondo, *"The Life-Changing Magic of Tidying Up: The Japanese Art of Decluttering and Organizing"*, 2014.

It's hard to let go,
but that's where growth happens.

When we let go of negativity, we create space. It is a liberating act that opens us to receive. We become open to noticing beauty and miracles, expressing gratitude and experiencing joy all around us.

Letting go leads to clarity. Clarity clears a new pathway for shafts of new light to flow. New insights and larger breakthroughs become easier to see. It opens the floodgates of growth and discovery.

The Liberating Power of Letting Go
Reflection Questions

What do you choose to hold on to in your life?

Are there some opportunities for letting go and liberating yourself? What past relationships, activities, fixed thinking, limiting beliefs, and other things in your life have you been holding on to that are no longer serving you well?

Review your possessions. What things in your life give you joy? What things have outlived their useful life? What is the difference between sacred, and sentimental, for you?

Review your current commitments and activities. Are these still providing the intended purpose for you?

When beginning a new year, season, or chapter in your life, while saying goodbye to the old, is there anything else you'd like to leave behind with it?

The Power of Forgiveness

To forgive is to set a prisoner free and
discover that the prisoner was you.

Lewis Smedes

No matter how high up the executive flagpole we've been in our careers, each of us experiences pain when we get hurt. When we encounter difficult circumstances, such as being passed over for a promotion, or a job loss, we may feel a range of emotions, such as disappointment, hurt, rejection, and anger. We may feel harshly or unfairly treated by others. Often these events happen within the context of unhealthy corporate cultures that may be bureaucratic and impersonal. There may have been internal politics, backstabbing, or cold hearted ruthlessness in treating employees as disposable assets.

At times it feels like nothing seems fair. The resulting resentment, anger, or hurt can consume substantial amounts of mental energy. It's hard to resist the temptations to feel victimized, or fight back.

We are faced with a critical moment that requires us to make a decision.

While acknowledging there are real injustices that do occur that require us to pursue a response to protect our interests or legal rights, we need to reflect on several important questions.

Do we want to carry negative baggage with us? Do we want to concede the future to the pain of the past? Do we want to surrender power and control of our life to others? And if we choose to do so, for how long?

Unresolved hurt can evolve to harbored anger that invades the body. A seed germinates within and begins to burrow below the surface, takes root and grows. It gathers strength as it bores a deeper and deeper hole until it becomes hardened bitterness that gets covered up and protected by a heavily fortified wall of defense. The hurt inside occupies space in the deep recesses in the back of the brain and becomes harder and harder to find over time. It may be out of sight, but it is not out of mind. It becomes heavy baggage that weighs you down on your journeys.

As long as you harbor these negative feelings inside you and don't transform them into constructive energy to move on, you'll concede the future to the past. You might think that suppressing your anger so that it doesn't plague you is a good way to move on. It is not because you will still be affected if you don't transform your anger into peace.

An alternative option is forgiveness. Forgiveness is a powerful, intentional, selfish act that we undertake for our own peace and serenity.

In *"The Art of Forgiving"*[17], Lewis Smedes describes forgiveness as a process with three steps. First, we recognize the flawed humanity of those who hurt us. Then, we surrender our right to get even. We begin to wish them well. Understand that forgiving does not mean that we have to restore the past relationship, nor continue to allow ourselves to remain open for further abuse. It does not require or expect the person who hurt you to apologize or to make amends. We can wish them well and still release them back to the sea of humanity.

Forgiveness is a powerful, intentional, selfish act we undertake for our own peace and serenity.

Letting go of the painful past isn't easy. But it's harder to look forward positively if you haven't. The key is to become intentional about using past career and life experiences to your advantage. When you examine what happened, what are the lessons you learned? Write them down. It makes a tremendous difference.

Begin to practice the art of forgiving by always remembering human frailties. Refuse to concede the future by giving power to the painful past. Try to forgive those who have harmed you for the hurt they inflicted. Life is filled with incredible beauty. Forgiveness sets you free to experience it. It's a powerful, liberating process that takes time and requires patience. It's a decision and a choice that YOU make for YOU.

---

[17] Lewis B. Smedes, *"The Art of Forgiving: When You Need to Forgive and Don't Know How"*, 1996.

The Power of Forgiveness
Reflection Questions

Letting go of the past isn't easy. The key is to become intentional about using past career and life experiences to your advantage. Think of an experience where someone hurt you. Write it down, it makes a tremendous difference.

What exactly was done to you? Did you develop unrealistic expectations? Did you remain in a situation you could have left?

Examine what you've learned from the person who harmed you. No one is entirely bad or good. Don't focus only on the hurts but make a list of all the things this person taught you. Assess the positives, such as experiences, accomplishments and new relationships formed.

We can even assess negatives in a positive, constructive light. When you examine what happened what are the lessons you learned?

Seeing Light through

the Forest and Trees

Are You Keeping

the Big Picture in Mind?

The greatest attribute a producer can have is the ability to see the whole picture. Most artists, when they record something, don't listen to the whole thing. They listen to what they're doing. When the music is played back, he'll be listening to himself. The producer must sit back, view the whole thing in perspective and make sense of it.

George Martin

Every so often it is helpful for a leader to climb to the mountaintop and look out from the summit to survey the big picture horizon. What lies ahead as far as the eye can see? Am I, or we as a team, heading the right direction? Is everyone positioned where they are supposed to be?

What is the big picture purpose? Do I have clarity about this? How frequently do I assess where I am from both the forest and trees perspective? How do I know when it's time to make a course correction?

When emotionally hooked or triggered, feeling overrides thinking. When in a hyper feeling state, leaders lose clarity of thinking, narrow their focus, and ruminate.

When triggered, one of the very best questions someone can ask is, "Are you keeping the big picture in mind?"

Are you keeping the big picture in mind?
When emotionally hooked or triggered,
slowing down to reflect can remind
and redirect to the present, bring thinking
back online, and widen focus.

Like Google Maps, there are benefits from zooming up to look at the larger picture perspective. How big a deal is this situation? How significant is the issue? What difference will this make 30 days from now? A year from now?

Even a little reduction in emotional reactivity is healthy and can reduce the intensity, frequency, and duration of a trigger. Redirecting to the present by keeping the big picture in mind widens focus for considering other important questions.

Are You Keeping the Big Picture in Mind?
Reflection Questions

How frequently do you assess where you are, from both the forest and trees perspective?

When you look at the horizon, what lies ahead, as far as the eye can see? Are you (or we) heading the right direction? Is everyone positioned where they're supposed to be? Do you (we) need a course correction?

When emotionally triggered: Are you giving power away for someone to hijack your life right now? What are you thinking? What are you feeling?

What difference will this make on my life longer term? How important will this be in 30 days, or a year from now? Is this a defining moment in my life?

Finding Bliss in the Mundane

*I felt so relaxed. It just felt very easy, and that's why
it surprised me that I had broken my world record.*

Katie Ledecky

While Olympic swimmer Katie Ledecky was in the pool blowing away her competition, extending her lead throughout the race on the way to shattering her own world record in the 800 meter event, the announcer declared she could swim even longer distance races if they were held. She found "bliss in the mundane". Katie sustains her powerful swimming stroke and settles into an unrelenting pace for so long, because she loves swimming.

My daughter runs half-marathons several times a year. She settles into her pace, listens to inspiring music that energizes her, and goes with the flow. She enjoys the training discipline of preparation, and fulfilling accomplishment of completing her goals on big day events. She loves running.

I have another friend who plays bass guitar in a rock band. He goes with the flow of the music and can set a groove for hours. He loves playing bass guitar.

Leaders clarify and cultivate meaningful work by tapping into or refreshing what they love to do. I've met leaders who light up like a Christmas tree when sharing their love of cloud computing, or their fulfillment in real estate portfolio management, innovating and creating new products and services, helping customers and clients solve problems.

Being clear and comfortable expressing what you love to do does not diminish your executive presence. It enhances it.

People believe you when you speak from the heart.

Finding Bliss in the Mundane
Reflection Questions

How did you first discover your field? Who or what opened a channel of curiosity and sparked your interest in pursuing your functional expertise (sales, marketing, finance, IT. . .)? The industry you work? Your career path?

What do you love about the work you do right now?

Where do you lose track of time and don't want it to end?

What hobbies, interests, and activities spring joy, refresh, or inspire you?

Where do you find "bliss in the mundane"?

You Decide Good Enough

Be true to yourself. Make each day a masterpiece.
Help others. Drink deeply from good books.
Make friendship a fine art.
Build a shelter against a rainy day.

John Wooden

Everyone has a plan until they get punched in the mouth.

Mike Tyson

It can be exhilarating to get a lot of work done, and feel a genuine sense of accomplishment as we climb the corporate ladder. There are periods in our career and life when it's time to push hard. When you love what you're doing, feeling fulfilled and energized, go with the flow. It's ok if you love working long hours as you pursue and achieve goals important to you. You've been thoughtful and aware of your choices, understand the sacrifices and recognize the tradeoffs you're making.

A leader was promoted to a new role overseeing an office with 200 employees. She brought many strengths to her new position. She was respected by her colleagues for her very strong technical subject matter expertise, solving complex problems and managing transactions. She was acknowledged for her positive energy and contagious enthusiasm, and successful track record building high value relationships, growth, and navigating change throughout her career.

Stepping up into her new role quickly revealed two development goals. The first was managing added complexity. Adjusting to her many new responsibilities, juggling competing priorities, and managing heavy client demands and difficult personalities resulted in overwhelm.

Staring at the challenge in front of her, she said, "I'm trying to do fifty things today!" So much to do, needing to stay on task, staying up late each night. Activity was well past her saturation point. Her overcommitting and underestimating time to complete work resulted in scrambling to meet deadlines. It was a never ending battle, struggling to get enough done each and every day.

The second development goal was building confidence. The leader was trying to control and do everything herself, and had been doubting herself with negative self-talk ("I can't" . . . "I won't" . . . "I don't . . . "I'm not" . . .). Worn down tired and energy depleted, she was becoming reactive when dealing with negative surprises. She put additional pressure on herself and kept things bottled inside. She shared "I've been beating myself up for twenty years!"

The leader wanted to develop better habits and routines to stay strong, calm, and positive in the midst of challenges. She wanted more urgency focus, vs. unproductive worry in order to control what she could and let go the rest. She wanted to be there for family and important life events.

We discussed the scarcity mindset. This is a common experience shared by too many leaders, of "not enough". They begin the day already feeling tired and not getting enough sleep. The day ends with exhaustion and feeling unfulfilled from not getting enough done.

What would it take for you to shift, from "not enough" to "good enough"?

Who is the arbiter of what's good enough? The intrinsic motivation of taking ownership with clarity and confidence in knowing that YOU are the decider in your own life makes a huge difference. When you take control, you define what's good enough. You define the game and commitment each day. Balance optimism with reality testing to evaluate where you are. By knowing your saturation and tipping point, you can say no when asked to commit to take on another task when that puts everything at risk.

You are the arbiter of what's good enough. What does success look like, aligned with your values?

You Decide Good Enough
Reflection Questions

What would it take for you to shift from "not enough" to "good enough"?

Who is the arbiter of what's good enough for each day?

Conquering Overwhelm

The secret of getting ahead is getting started.
The secret of getting started is breaking your complex
overwhelming tasks into small, manageable tasks,
and then starting on the first one.

Mark Twain

Whenever I hear a leader share that he or she is overwhelmed, we do not seek to add anything else to the already full "to do" list. We explore options for letting go. Identify what's most important and focus on fewer things on the plate each day. We address delegating some of the pile vs. overcommitting and setting unrealistic expectations for a busy, full day.

A leader of a global, complex, multi-billion dollar company has a daily practice that enables her to manage her very full day. It involves staying connected with her intuition, and remaining focused and fulfilled. Her silence and solitude time is important, non-negotiable space. It is "against the law" for anyone to disturb her for the first half hour when she arrives in the office. The first thing she does each morning is spend quiet time centering on her four big picture objectives. She decides on four specific actions she will accomplish by the end of the day ahead.

The drive for success, wealth accumulation, or power is a hideous trap. Intense focused, we can get tunnel-visioned, lost in the trees and not see the forest. We get used to running at a hectic pace throughout the week, then spend the weekend working even more, or cramming our schedules with a slug of personal activities.

Choosing and balancing priorities is different for everyone. There isn't a black box answer applicable for all. I've met many extremely wealthy people with no semblance of balance in their lives, or happiness either. The same goes for people striving to gain power or control over others.

One of the most common issues I encounter with executives is their experience of being overwhelmed, juggling and prioritizing tasks. They are managing complexity and processing massive volumes of data, all while maintaining a high need for insightful thinking and knowing the deep importance of building and maintaining relationships. I've interviewed leaders and teams in the midst of being tasked with upwards of twenty significant complex projects and initiatives to be completed within the next six months.

A lengthy pile of tasks can freeze us right in our tracks. Several executives have shared feeling frustration at running hard yet experiencing exasperation that nothing ever seems to get done. When I ask them what they're trying to accomplish today, often I hear responses like "I'm trying to do 50 things today".

I follow up by asking them to estimate how long it would take for them to complete every task on their "to do" list.

Many leaders have shared it would take a month to complete the things they're trying to do today! Is it any wonder that feels like overwhelm?

There are solutions. Neuroscience research indicates that our brains can hold and manage up to seven items when clearly focused. When experiencing heavy stress, the number decreases to three or four. Leaders can reflect on the day ahead and choose 3 or 4 intentional goals or tasks to complete that will be good enough for today.

Leaders can estimate the time requirements for each task and be aware if they have space and flexibility to allow for unexpected events, distractions, and leadership opportunities that may arise. If one task is estimated to require eight hours, leaders can choose to limit goals to that one and also recognize they do not have much flexibility for anything else that day.

Maybe one or two are behavioral, or "being" development goals. What's on your "to be" list? For example, choosing to be joyful today, or being grateful even if we encounter a negative surprise. We can choose to be open, present, or aware today. Cheerful. Confident. Calm. Authentic. Self-compassionate. Empathic. Flexible. Light. Pick one or two that will serve you well. That will stretch you to develop and grow. Behavior goals often have far more impact and significance.

A leader of a rapidly growing business shared his daily discipline practice for managing the complexity of the day. Each morning he arrives in his office, his very first action is to take a square post-it note and jot down four things he chooses that will get done today. Most days, at least one of those goals is a leadership objective checking in with someone on his team. He also sets a time boundary for his commitment at work.

At the end of the day he tosses the post-it note away before leaving the office. He lets go of the past and retires home to rest and re-energize for the next morning.

This daily practice of working in "threes and fours", choosing tasks to accomplish leads to quantifiable, tangible results, along with a sense of fulfillment. If we are able to successfully complete just three important things a day and apply simple math, how many important tasks can we complete in a typical 5-day week? Doesn't that equate to 15 important things we've accomplished in a week? And over a four-week period, can we look back to see we've accomplished 60 significant goals or tasks in a month?

Conquering Overwhelm
Reflection Questions

What are three or four overarching, big picture goals for this year, or season in your life or career?

What are three or four tasks or behaviors that will be good enough for today?

What's on your "to be" list, behaviors or "being" goals?

What is the estimated time for each task, and boundary for the day overall? Do you have flexibility space for unexpected events today?

How do you assess what to say "yes" to? Even more important, are you choosing what to say "no" to?

How Long Does it Take

to Do a One Hour Task?

Urgency sharpens focus.

Lou Holtz

The answer to this question seems obvious. How long *should* it take to do a one hour task? One hour.

How long *does* it take? Our actions and behaviors often indicate otherwise.

Research studies have shown that the average worker typically has consistent focus on a task for just three to eleven minutes before we are interrupted by either an external or internal distraction. External distractions include incoming emails, phone calls, or someone knocking on our door seeking requests for assistance, counsel, or wanting to engage in the banter of the day. Internal distractions are our self-chatter . . . I'm hungry . . . what's happening later . . . a recent argument with someone . . . did I leave the coffee pot on when I left the house?

After the interruption or distraction, how long does it take to get back in the right frame of mind and return to the original task? Research indicates the gap in time is twenty-five minutes, IF I return to the task at all!

Based on this data, how long does it take then to do a one hour task? We focus on a task at hand for 3-11 minutes . . . a distraction . . . a 25 minute gap (IF we return at all!) . . . another 3-11 minutes on task . . . distraction . . . a 25 minute gap . . . another 3-11 minutes on task . . .

Is it any wonder it often feels like it takes several hours to get a simple task done?

There are solutions and options. When seeing or hearing the sound of an incoming email, why do many of us automatically stop and disrupt concentration to look? It gets attention and highest priority, it jumps to the front of the line. Often it turns out to be a spam message or low priority note that does not require immediate response.

What about that knock on the door? Is this a distraction, a leadership opportunity, or both? What are some options? For example, when someone knocks on the door asking if we have a moment, unless it is a truly urgent matter that requires immediate attention, one option might be a polite but firm no. We are not available right now, and look for another time to meet later. Another answer may be yes, we have a moment. But only a moment. If this is going to take longer than a minute or two, we'll need to meet at a time when we're both present and focused.

With self-awareness, discipline, and practice, leaders can choose to be more intentional in the present. Leaders can sharpen focus on what's most important and reduce distractions to be more efficient in accomplishing tasks. Leaders can even complete one hour tasks – in an hour!

How Long Does it Take to Do a One Hour Task?
Reflection Questions

How long does it take for you to do a one-hour task?

What are some examples of external distractions that get in the way?

What are some examples of internal distractions that hinder progress?

Sometimes You Need

to Take Breaks!

Almost everything will work again if you unplug
It for a few minutes . . . including you.

Ann Lamott

Whenever we're feeling stuck and seeking new insights, neuroscience research suggests breakthroughs happen when four factors are present: 1) when we are quiet, 2) inward focused in a reflective state, 3) slightly positive, and 4) not focused on the problem.

One evening early in my days becoming an entrepreneur I was conflicted. I was being pulled in two different directions. Some people were pushing hard for me to commit to a very risky venture project that would require my full attention over the next several months. I would have to turn down some other standing commitments and cease pursuing any other income generating opportunities in order to comply with their requirements. There was no middle ground option for consideration.

The pressure was on as I sat at the dinner table across from my ten year old daughter and eight year old son. I was on parenting detail, my wife and eldest daughter were elsewhere. We were eating in sheer silence. I was stuck, immersed in the problem, racking my brain, agonizing what to do next, when my young daughter stared at me and asked a curious question:

She asked, "Do you ever notice how much quieter it is when people are missing?"

Jarred back to present, I gave her the most logical, obvious response in the moment. "Well, if two people are missing, then yes, it's about 40% quieter." Unconvinced, and undeterred, she replied, "No, it's a lot quieter than that!" With zero table conversation, it was *100%* quieter!

My kids were witnessing their father in the midst of wrestling with a dilemma. I did not want to concern them, but they noticed anyway. Busted, I confessed to both of them that I was having a very hard time sorting out a problem, and struggling to make a decision. I just could not figure out what to do.

My ten-year old daughter listened and replied firmly, with confidence: "That's why you need to take breaks!"

When your heart is open to listen,
breakthroughs, "aha" moments,
and answers you seek can come
anywhere, anytime, from anyone.

Empathic listening is opening your heart to hear another. Some answers we seek come from usual suspects like the leaders, counselors, mentors, and subject matter experts. If you're listening, you may even hear wisdom coming from anyone who crosses your path. It may be a coffee barista, a neighbor walking their dog encouraging you to have a nice day, or your own child reminding you to take breaks.

When the student is ready, the teacher will appear. As the parent, I thought I was the dispenser of wisdom. That day, my young daughter was my messenger, providing profound counsel right when I needed it.

After finishing dinner, the three of us went outside and played in the backyard together. We tossed a frisbee around for an hour. We laughed.

I sat quietly in my room for a few moments as my children prepared themselves for bed that evening. Feeling very grateful, and at peace, for the first time in what seemed like ages, the clear answer that had been so elusive flooded right into my head. The next morning I made a confident decision that was right for me and my family. One I have never regretted since.

Sometimes You Need to Take Breaks!
Reflection Questions

When do your breakthroughs, aha moments and new insights most often happen for you? What are some of the factors that help you set the conditions for success?

When are you most quiet?

When are you in an inward focused in a reflective state?

What helps you be slightly positive?

What do you do to step away from the problem?

When, and how frequently, do you take breaks?

Light Practices

Discernment from Chaos to Clarity

There is a hard truth to be told: before spring becomes
beautiful, it is plug ugly, nothing but mud and muck.
I have walked in the early spring through fields
that will suck your boots off, a world so wet and woeful
it makes you yearn for the return of ice.
But in that muddy mess, the conditions for
rebirth are created.

Parker Palmer

Discernment tools and processes can be useful for simplifying complexity, conquering overwhelm, navigating change and transition, brainstorming new ideas, problem solving and making critical decisions.

The goal of discernment is to get clarity for
making confident decisions and taking action.
Creating space by altering pace,
gathering information, reflecting, prioritizing,
and choosing the next steps as you are led.

Distilling New Information

Distilling truth from overwhelming amounts of information is the essence of leadership.

Carly Fiorina

Step 1 – Brainstorm. Stream of consciousness, let all ideas and thoughts come. Pour out and gather into a container document, post it notes on flip charts, or other format that gathers the aggregate data.

Step 1A – Before moving to next step, be content to dwell for a while. Have you collected all readily available data? Be Ok with continuing to receive additional new information that comes.

Step 2 – Organize. Assemble the aggregate data into a coherent whole. Identify common themes and categories.

Step 2A – Step back and ask: Is that it? Be content to dwell until ready to proceed.

Step 3 – Edit and sharpen for clarity. Distill and edit the data into the story you want to own. Let this come, don't move until ready and led to share.

Evaluating "Either/Or",

or "Go, or No Go" Decisions

Should I stay or should I go?

The Clash

Assessing the benefits and consequences for taking, or not taking, action:

Step 1 – On a blank sheet of paper, create four boxes by drawing a vertical line down the center of the page, and a horizontal line as well.

Step 2 – Label the boxes on the page as follows:

Upper left =
"Benefits taking action"

Upper right =
"Consequences taking action"

Lower left =
"Benefits NOT taking action"

Lower right =
"Consequences NOT taking action"

Step 3 – Focus on one box at a time. Reflect and capture all ideas, thoughts, feelings, concerns related to that box. Not all boxes need to have the same number of items, some factors will have more importance.

Example – Asking for and Receiving Feedback

Benefits of asking	Consequences of asking
Learn what's working	- Might hear something hard to hear
Strengths; blind spots	- Might not like what I hear
Suggestions for	- How will I react?
improvement	- How will this be used, or
Identify development goals	goals documented?

Benefits NOT asking	Consequences NOT asking
Stay in my comfort zone	- Lack awareness of key market data
Focus on current goals	
Can ask later	- Blind spots remain blind
	- Wonder what others see

Making Urgent, Critical, Confident Decisions

May your choices reflect your hopes, not your fears.

Nelson Mandela

Step 1 – Sleep on it

Step 2 – Go for a walk or run, get away from the problem

Step 3 – Be with your family or important people in your life. Envision how this decision or choice will impact them.

Step 4 – Seek counsel or input from anyone you want.
Important caveat: No one person should be given power or authority to function as a guru or Svengali with undue influence or control over you to tell you what to do, or how you should live your life.

Step 5 – Sit in a favorite chair and reflect. Be patient, content to dwell, don't rush the process or move until you have clarity and led to take next steps. There may well be some dissonance. That's what makes it a hard decision vs. the easy ones. Absolute certainty is not the goal, just your best sense given the factors. What will it take to make a confident decision?

Discernment from Chaos to Clarity
Reflection Questions

Think of a recent pending decision, or action you are contemplating now.

What are the benefits of taking action now? What are the potential consequences of taking action now?

What are the benefits of NOT taking action now? What are the potential consequences of NOT taking action now?

Discernment Process Checklist – Have you:

Slept on it?
Gone for a walk, run, (away from the problem)?
Been with family or important people in your life?
Sought counsel or input from anyone you want?
Sat in a chair and reflected until you have clarity?

What is emerging for you?
What do you need to make a confident decision?

Navigating a Busy Season

There are only the pursued, the pursuing,
the busy and the tired.

F. Scott Fitzgerald

Busy seasons can often seem overwhelming and exhausting. Rather than just capitulating to all the demands and competing priorities, there are options and choices for being intentional in navigating a busy season and focusing on what's important for positive growth.

Here are some practices shared by successful leaders who have experienced positive results and personal peak performance for themselves and their teams heading into, or in the midst of, navigating busy seasons:

Upfront planning. Setting goals to meet our commitments for big picture growth and productivity targets. Sharing the vision, aligning the team, and challenging each other to collaborate and communicate. Creating agendas that are organized and timely, with an expressed goal to reduce the number of late nights burning the midnight oil or last minute fire drills.

Leaders ask everyone on the team for their buy-in. Is everyone on board with our plan? With buy-in, another important leadership opportunity is to ask each team member to share their individual growth goals. Awareness and understanding enables leaders to feed and facilitate the hopes and dreams of each individual on the team.

Build in flexibility. Even with the best laid plans, the unexpected happens. Leaders can anticipate late negative surprises. Clients delay providing critical information on a timely basis, due to their own priorities or disorganization. Some people prefer to be more organized, while others prefer to be more adaptable and flexible. Untimely life events happen. People get sick. Daily distractions or leadership opportunities to mentor and provide guidance happen throughout the day. There are some who will be late in responding to the call.

When leaders plan for late negative surprises, they don't throw us off stride when they surface. Leaders can recognize them and choose to be less reactive. They can lean into and engage the surprise. If late negative surprises don't come, the possibility of a late *positive* surprise opens up. We're done early!

Identify good enough. Instead of experiencing overwhelm from staring at the lengthy and never ending "to do" list, identify three or four of the most important priorities and tasks to accomplish today. You are the arbiter of what's good enough each day.

With focused attention on the important tasks, several leaders have shared that they find themselves coming up for air earlier than expected, having completed their chosen tasks for the day. When this happens there are choices. Some spend time worrying they must be doing something wrong or missing something to find themselves in this position! Some choose to get a jump on tomorrow and do additional tasks within the time boundary for the day. Some simply appreciate the temporary breather, content and grateful in the moment.

Boundaries and rest. What is my time commitment today? 10 hours, 12 hours, 14? How long is enough? How will I recognize when it's time to take a break during the day, and stop to build strength and freshen for the next day? Successive long days and late evening pushes, with intensive concentration, require recovery time. Depleted energy weakens our defenses, compromises our thinking, and makes us more susceptible to be reactive with shorter triggers and heightened anxieties, fears, and concerns.

At the end of the workweek, many celebrate Friday by fleeing jobs for weekend fun time. TGIF. Days away from work are often crammed wall to wall with a full schedule of family commitments, errands, and other activities. No doubt leaders need to switch off the hard driving pace of a busy, full workweek for a break, time to rest and recharge their batteries. Imagine what it would feel like to thank God for Monday. TGIM. Hitting the ground running, feeling energized. Returning to a job we loved, not consumed 24/7 but engaged and enjoying it when we arrived.

Know your tipping point. As a committed team player, leaders challenge themselves to contribute and be willing to take on work. It is important to be optimistic. It is also important to balance optimism with reality checking, and know there is a saturation point where, if another task is taken on, the additional burden will put the whole portfolio of commitments and responsibilities at risk. Leaders raise their hand and ask for help when they hit a space beyond their subject matter expertise or endurance limits. They know how and when to say no.

Acknowledge and celebrate successes. Notice people doing excellence, catch them doing well in the act and tell them. Actively practice gratitude. Foster friendships. One of the best indicators of retention is building friendships in the workplace. It's hard to leave an organization when you genuinely enjoy the company of working alongside friends in the midst of executing the workload.

Keep your sense of humor. Lighten up. Remember Rule #6: Don't take yourself so seriously. Loosen up and move, find laughter, play some anthem songs that keep you energized, strong and resilient.

Have a process for frequently checking in. Develop a regular check-in to assess status, manage complexity, lead teams and manage ourselves for awareness and focus during busy seasons:

Step 1 – Assess the big picture. Get out of the weeds and look from the forest perspective. Review the current status for the whole mission, project, or portfolio of projects. Are we where we want to be right now? Are we heading in the right direction? Do we need to make a course correction?

Step 2 – Assess current short-term goals and intentions. Long "to do" lists can be intimidating. What are the most important 3-4 tasks or objectives to accomplish today? What is the boundary for today (is it 8 hours? 10 hours? 14?) You are the arbiter of what's good enough. What can you control, what can you let go of today?

Step 3 – Assess the status of your team. Frequently check in with every member on the team. What are their priorities for this week? Do they have clarity about this? How can I help? What do they need? When are next milestones or deadlines? Are we communicating commitments and expectations clearly, and in alignment? Is anything getting in the way or holding them back? What are their next steps?

Upfront planning, flexibility, identifying good enough, setting boundaries, rest, knowing tipping points, celebrating success, and keeping a sense of humor will enable positive results in navigating a busy season.

A leader with over twenty years leading teams through busy seasons recently shared with me his numbers were great. His team was working hard and efficient, he had never been more proud of them. Fulfilled and energized, he proclaimed "This is the best busy season of my life!"

Navigating a Busy Season
Reflection Questions

How do you engage upfront planning before entering a busy season? How do you insure everyone is on board? What are team goals for growth and fulfillment? What are growth and development goals for each individual?

How do you plan for "late negative surprises"?

Assess the big picture. Review the current status for the whole mission, project, or portfolio of projects. Are you where you want to be right now? What are the next milestone commitment dates or deadlines? Are you headed in the right direction, or need a course correction?

Assess current short-term commitments. What are three or four most important goals to accomplish today? What is your time commitment today? How will you recognize when it's time to take a break during the day, and stop?

Check in with the team. Are we clearly communicating commitments and expectations? What are their priorities this week? Do they have clarity? What do they need? Have you recently noticed and acknowledged excellence, actively practiced gratitude with your team?

Asking for, Receiving, and Responding to Feedback

Constant development is the law of life, and a man who always tries to maintain his dogmas in order to appear consistent drives himself into a false position.

Mahatma Gandhi

Early in my career, I was known for being a hard charging leader with relentless tenacity for getting things done. I was responsible for leading and growing a large regional practice and driving results. I enjoyed being acknowledged and seen this way, which reinforced my intentions and behaviors. I hoped this mindset served as an example of excellence to follow and emulate.

When the firm conducted an upward feedback survey, I was not concerned. I had been acknowledged as an inspirational leader and positive mentor in many other situations. I expected to hear my team respected me for my dedication and commitment, saw me as tough, but fair, and enjoyed working with, learning, and growing from me.

It was difficult to receive upward feedback from the team that I was being too hard on them. My unrelenting tenacity was experienced and translated as overly critical, micro-managing, and reactive to mistakes or bad news. This news surprised me. I didn't need to be liked, but it wasn't my desire to be a hard driving micro-manager who no one wanted to work with either. It was a splash of water that opened my eyes and revealed a blind spot. I was awaken to stop, reflect, and clarify the leader I aspired to be, and identify steps for positive growth and change.

It takes courage to seek and ask for constructive feedback. It takes courage for people who know you well to provide it. In my coaching practice I conduct informational interviews to gather 360 feedback from a series of reviewers who know the leader well. The goal is to identify a consensus view of how others around the leader see and experience them. To enable people to share freely and anonymously, no one is quoted or cited. Consensus comments are shared without attribution.

An executive leading manufacturing and production of medical devices in a life science company received feedback that he was micromanaging and hard on people. He had an uncompromising value for product quality, because if the device failed, people died. It was his way or the highway. No discussion, disagreements or dissent tolerated.

When the consensus feedback was shared with him, the debriefing consultant called him on his reaction in the moment. She said "I can see you're trying to figure out who it was who said this about you. I want you to hear this: It isn't one person who sees you this way. It's nine out of ten!"

Then she opened his eyes to the awareness of the leadership challenge: "If you can't see it, you can't fix it!"

While debriefing the data can be initially difficult for the leader, the collective input received from colleagues reveal special insights. They are gifts from your team to you. Individuals on the team share how they see and experience you. They share their perspectives of the strengths you demonstrate and identify development opportunities.

What's the upside to receiving feedback? This important data opens awareness, provides options for consideration, and helps sharpens the leader's focus for growth and development. In addition to identifying blind spots and derailing behaviors, leaders can also solicit feedback to understand what's working well, how they are helping others, and identify examples of what should continue.

What's the downside to not being open to receiving feedback? The leader will be unaware of any blind spot(s) or derailing behaviors that are getting in the way of their success. Leaders will also be less aware of positive actions and behaviors that impact individuals and the team. Additionally, they will miss opportunities to improve communication.

How will you receive and use feedback to clarify your goals, and identify next action steps to grow as a leader?

What are some growth opportunities and options for receiving and responding to feedback?

An initial step is to acknowledge the contribution of people who provide honest, well intentioned feedback. It takes courage to give, and it takes courage to receive. We can thank anyone and everyone for providing feedback.

Leaders can share how they have reflected on the input. They can share insights and development goals that they've identified. With authenticity and humility, they can affirm their desire to grow as a leader. Leaders can invite the team's continued participation and welcome ongoing support as they practice and assimilate new behaviors.

Leaders can ask others to share their own growth goals, and what they want to accomplish working on the mission and with the team. With clarity and awareness of what's important to all, leaders can nurture mutual growth and take positive next steps toward everyone's leadership and professional aspirations.

Asking for, Receiving, and Responding to Feedback
Reflection Questions

How do you want to be seen and experienced as a leader?

How do you become aware of and learn how others experience you?

How will you use feedback to clarify your goals, and identify next action steps to grow as a leader?

Active Gratitude

Gratitude changes the pangs of memory
into a tranquil joy.

Dietrich Bonhoeffer

When I ask leaders how they practice gratitude in the workplace, many examples surface. Tangible recognitions in performance reviews, cash rewards and bonuses, taking people to lunch, and informal expressions of thanks are ways to acknowledge efforts and jobs well done.

An inspirational leader I interviewed for my first book shared an event that began a life practice of expressing gratitude. A few years ago, some friends had passed away in her life. Time flies quickly in a busy world, especially when one is dedicated and focused on professional goals, meeting deadlines and completing tasks. She agonized about not having told people, who meant so much to her, how much they had impacted her life. She was awakened to take corrective action going forward.

She made a list of several people who had made a positive impact on her life with whom she wanted to meet.

The first person was a doctor she had met much earlier, during a period of discouragement. He had changed her life forever, but she had never taken the time to tell him. She met with him and shared how grateful she was for how he had helped redirect her life course.

As she began meeting with others, her gratitude list kept growing. It soon became so long there was no time to meet everyone individually. Some may have been tempted to give up the practice at this point. Undeterred, she came up with a creative solution and started meeting three people at a time. She expressed her gratitude with each in front of the others, sharing how they had impacted her life.

Eventually word got out about what she was doing. A friend lent her a home with a stunning view, overlooking the ocean, to throw a gratitude party. She invited twenty people, from different places and periods of her life, including some professional colleagues, many friends, and her mother. Guests arrived at the event thinking they would know everyone, but stepped into the room to discover they knew no one else. Going in reverse chronological order, she shared how each individual had impacted her life and expressed her profound gratitude. Taking her time, she addressed each person, one by one, twenty times over, finally landing at her mother. By the time she was done, everybody knew everybody.

Sharing gratitude stories is contagious and expands our thinking about the power of the practice of expressing gratitude. Good things happen when leaders reflect and share examples of who best models inspirational leadership. Positive action steps emerge.

When leaders compile a list of leaders who have served as role model examples for them, they can reach out to each one to share how they have made a positive impression and express their gratitude.

> *We can always find light practicing gratitude, acknowledging people who have made a positive difference in our lives.*

After a group conversation about the power of active gratitude with an executive team, a leader shared something that had happened as follow up. In an all hands office meeting with over a hundred people in attendance, a senior executive had called out a director.

Many expect the worst when singled out by a superior in a public office meeting forum. Instead, in front of everyone present, he declared, "I saw how you interacted with the customer, how you led your team, excelled in completing the work project, rebuilt and saved that important client relationship. And I have never told you how grateful I am for what you've done."

The leader who shared this incident with me said, "I've worked with this guy over 25 years. I have never seen him do anything like this before. When the meeting ended I went up to him and asked why he had done it, and he replied he was just actively practicing gratitude. I told him how impressed I was with what he had done, and that we would all be so much more effective if we did this more often."

Active Gratitude
Reflection Questions

How do you practice gratitude in life, and in the workplace?

Who was it that first saw leadership qualities in you, planted a seed, and encouraged your success?

Who best models for you what confidence, enthusiasm, and passion for their work look like?

Who best exemplifies calm under pressure?

Who shows you what resilience looks like, bouncing back from setbacks and disappointments?

Reflect on what this person means to you and how they have made a positive impact on your life. Reach out to connect, and schedule time to meet. Look them in the eye and share with them the impact they've had on your life.

Fill Your Calendar with People

Who Fill Your Life

Sometimes our light goes out, but is blown again into instant flame by an encounter with another human being. Each of us owes the deepest thanks to those who have rekindled this inner light.

Dr. Albert Schweitzer

The friend in my adversity I shall always cherish most. I can better trust those who helped to relieve the gloom of my dark hours than those who are so ready to enjoy with me the sunshine of my prosperity.

Ulysses S. Grant

During times of heightened stress or pressure in our lives, we can get stuck in our problems and lose focus of the big picture. Life can get very serious. What happens to laughter and joy when we hunker down? Worry crowds it out. Sometimes worry can wipe the smile right off your face. We may even forget there are people nearby for support.

We do not thrive in isolation. We are not meant to muscle through life's hardships, or fight all our battles alone.

We can proactively schedule healthy activities that crowd out life draining negativity instead of getting immersed in it.

It is uplifting to look forward and see wonderful people approaching on the horizon. We set ourselves up for good things to happen when we include conversations with people who matter most to us.

This is especially rewarding when facing challenges, experiencing setbacks or falls, having a hard day, or preparing for important meetings when we want to show up and be experienced at our very best. Planting special people on our calendar brings joy and keeps us grounded.

An intentional practice of meeting positive people on our path provides healthy shots of energy that rejuvenates our spirit when we most need it.

We don't have to wait for others to call us, we can be the conduit who initiates action. We can choose who to reach out to and invite in to a conversation. Over the course of our lives we meet school friends, battle-tested teammates, former and current work colleagues, peers, respected competitors, mentors, and others who share common values and mutual interests. Some come into our lives for reasons, others for seasons, and some special kindred spirits endure for a life time.

Friends don't always tell us what we want to hear, but they do listen empathically, share thoughtful insights, offer perspectives and alternative points of view. We encourage and support each other, root for success, and offer cheer even when there is failure. We have each other's backs.

How about getting together occasionally to encourage and support each other?

We can mix it up and customize what works best, meet some at regular intervals, others more randomly, some in person, and others who live longer away distance by phone or Skype. This practice is not limited to special seasons of the year. We can be intentional, meeting special people in our lives, on an ongoing basis.

Celebrate life by affirming people in your life. Do not drive by this! Slow down to acknowledge and appreciate the blessings of friendship.

Fill Your Calendar with People Who Fill Your Life
Reflection Questions

Who shares your values and interests? Who helps you stay grounded?

Who best expresses optimism, gratitude, and joy? Who makes you laugh?

Who shows you what authenticity and courage look like? Who lives in their passion with relentless perseverance to pursue their hopes and dreams?

Who are the continuous learners who ask curious questions and enjoy sharing insights and perspectives?

Who encourages and supports you through the thrills, victories, and the agonies and defeats in life?

Who can you help, encourage and support today? Who is overdue for a catch up? Who are five people you can reach out to today and schedule a meeting or call to catch up in the next month?

Light at the End of the Day

Acknowledgments

No man is a failure if he has friends.[18]

Clarence

Many have come into my life with impact and significance. Some for reasons, some for seasons, some have endured a lifetime. I'm blessed and grateful for their seeing and believing in me, inviting me into their lives with opportunities to contribute. With head high and wide open heart I express my deepest gratitude:

To the leadership team at RSM, especially Don Natenstedt and Sam Mascareno for the trust and confidence you have placed in me. Being alongside your success supporting the growth and development of your leaders is one of my most fulfilling professional experiences.

To Chris, Chuck, Craig, Doyle, Darcy, George, Gretchen, InaMarie, Jeanne, Madelon, Pam, Rich, Ryan, Steve, and Tom, "iron sharpens iron" friends for amplifying your light, living your faith, encouragement and unwavering support.

---

[18] *"It's a Wonderful Life"*, 1946, quotes from imdb.com

To Christina, Claudia, Greg, Jamie, Megan, Sandy, and Susan, for peer coaching with aligned values of learning and continuous improvement. It warms the heart knowing we have each other's backs, root for each other when we stumble and fall, and never give up on anyone.

To Terry, for your life affirming, positive spirit, and showing us how to expand perspective for practicing gratitude. Your thoughtfulness and kindness means more than you know.

To inspirational leaders everywhere, especially the nineteen of you who graciously shared your hearts in my first book. You continue to show what authenticity looks like and invite us to be all in ourselves.

To Jim Harris and Perry Humphries, two of my dad's special lifelong friends and colleagues, who acknowledged a curious kid in the room, connected and built a friendship.

To music kindred spirits Terry, my Beatles compatriot and bodysurfing dolphin buddy; and Charles, for bringing light, kindness, and friendship in the darkest trials of navigating career transition. To Dave, Steve, and Curt, for friendship that has endured from school years, for fond memories of past glory days, and celebrating the present day, checking in sharing joys and struggles, keeping a sense of humor, and civility with respect when we passionately disagree.

To Arthur Hogarth Steele, aka "G-Daddy", my grandfather who showed me what humility and laughter looks like, taught me to always remember human frailties, and is sorely missed today. To cousins Fred, and Steve, for extending friendship beyond family.

To Chester and Susannah Noe, aka mom and dad, who taught me to keep a light touch and "do what's good for ya!" And my sister, Nancy Walker for a sibling rivalry blossoming to an adult friendship.

To my children, Emily, a natural, gifted teacher who shows how clarity and strength come from making good choices and taking breaks; Sean, whose curiosity, thoughtfulness and depth has led to new insights, perspectives and alternative points of view, and flexibility in letting go by going to the next pitch; and Theresa, with wisdom reminding when navigating difficult uncertain times to "Trust in the Lord with all your heart, and lean not on your own understanding." (Proverbs 3:5)

To my wife Pam, for loving support, partnership and companionship through many ups and downs, light and dark times, and guiding when in darkness to aim for light!

And lastly, to Cody, aka "the Ambassador of Goodwill", who always welcomes me home and reminds me I want to be as good a person as my dog already thinks I am.

January 28, 2019

About the Author

Randy Noe is an executive leadership coach who works with highly motivated leaders to elevate personal peak performance and sustain business growth. With more than 20 years senior leadership, operations, and finance experience, Randy brings perspective and best practices from working with thousands of C-level and VP leaders across all functions in companies of all sizes from small businesses to global companies. Randy understands pressures business leaders face because he's been there, speaks the language of business and leadership, and knows drivers that create and sustain business value.

Randy is an International Coach Federation (ICF) Professional Certified Coach and Mentor Coach, and Board Certified Coach, formally trained by the College of Executive Coaching.

Randy previously authored *Leading Well: The Essence of Wholehearted Inspirational Leaders* which explored emotional intelligence leadership themes from business leaders speaking candidly about lessons, challenges, and accomplishments that made them successful.

Contact Randy at: randy@randynoe.com
Website: www.randynoe.com

Made in the USA
Middletown, DE
10 February 2019